jason mraz love is a four l

MW00805624

contents

This book was approved by Jason Mraz

Artwork used with the permission of Atlantic Records
© 2012 Atlantic Recording Corporation
Artwork Direction & Design by Greg Burke

Transcribed by Jeff Jacobson

Cherry Lane Music Company
Director of Publications/Project Editor: Mark Phillips

ISBN 978-1-60378-959-2

Visit our website at www.cherrylaneprint.com

jason mraz love is a four letter word

Photo by Emily Shur

Jason Mraz spent 22 months on the road promoting *We Sing, We Dance, We Steal Things,* which followed his previous studio albums—the 2002 debut, *Waiting for My Rocket to Come,* and 2005's *Mr. A-Z.* "The tour was a blast and a whirlwind," he says. "I got turned on to the power of the voice and the power of the melody, and it created this desire in me to do it again immediately. Being able to inspire people and take a very simple message global gave me a preview of what that can do. I got home from the tour and thought, 'How can I spread love to the world through this new platform that I have?' That became my starting point for this new album." That album, *Love Is a Four Letter Word,* contains a heartfelt, uplifting collection that explores love's ups and downs, or, as Mraz puts it: "What one does in love to make it work, and what one does in love when it's time to let go."

Mraz had been writing steadily, putting all of his experiences into song. He eventually pared down to the final 12 that appear on his fourth studio album, *Love Is a Four Letter Word.* Recorded at Hollywood's legendary Sunset Sound with producer Joe Chiccarelli (White Stripes, Christina Perri) and a lineup of all-star session musicians, the album's clever arrangements and rich musical textures cushion the diamond-cut clarity of Mraz's pure tenor voice. "I feel like it showcases a variety of moods, from soulful baby-making-jams, to colorful new-jazz, to love-fueled acoustic-guitar-strokery, to rhythmic sunshine-pop," Mraz says. "And lyrically, I wanted the album to have a balance of the sacred and the silly because I want listeners to have both experiences. I want them to be able to go deep, but not get stuck there. I want them to have sunshine, but not get sunburned."

What ties the songs together is their theme. "I had this vision that the album was going to be called *Love* and I was going to talk about love and share love in one way or another," Mraz says. "I thought it was going to be easy because everything I write comes from a place of love, whether it's a new understanding of it, or a retelling of it, or a reawakening to it. But the more I looked at the subject, the more I realized that love almost can't be defined, and who am I to define it anyway? So I went on a journey to try to define the word and be an expression of it in the world."

That journey led to such songs as first single, "I Won't Give Up," an emotional acoustic-driven declaration that has already connected with the public, debuting at No. 1 on *Billboard*'s Digital Songs chart and topping the iTunes "Top Songs" and Hot AC radio charts. "It's about the experience I had with someone in which I had to go dark and let go of a lot things in order to see that I had everything already," Mraz says. Another movingly reflective moment is the hushed song of longing "In Your Hands," as well as "93 Million Miles," in which Mraz finds peace in the realization that you can feel at home in the world no matter where you are.

Fans of Mraz's upbeat, groove-fueled work will appreciate the feel-good "Everything Is Sound," which Mraz says was inspired by his love for Kirtan—a form of devotional call-and-response group singing in Sanskrit. "I had been going to several Kirtans around L.A. and wanted to write something with a bit of a chant in it so that people could just lose themselves a bit," he says. "I like the idea of sneaking some of that Hallelujah into contemporary pop music."

Other highlights include the breezy "Living in the Moment," the earthy story-song "Frank D. Fixer" (inspired by Mraz's grandfather), and the album's horn-driven opener "The Freedom Song," which was written by Seattle singer-songwriter Luc Reynaud. "Luc composed this song with some kids in a shelter in Baton Rouge after Hurricane Katrina and it was released on a CD called *Harmonic Humanity* and sold by homeless people as a way to raise money," Mraz explains. "When I heard it, I wrote to him and asked him if I could sing it for everyone I knew because it's important to keep the message going." During Mraz's 2010 trip to Ghana to work with anti-slavery organization Free the Slaves, he sang "The Freedom Song" at a school whose many students are former child slaves. The group has adopted it as its theme song.

It's that crossroads where music, love, hope, and giving back intersect that makes it all meaningful for Mraz, a dedicated surfer, yogi, and activist. Having worked with the Surfrider Foundation, Free the Slaves, and the True Colors Fund, as well as actively supporting VH1's Save the Music, Free the Children, SPARC (the School of the Performing Arts in the Richmond Community), MusiCares, and Life Rolls On, Mraz recently established the Jason Mraz Foundation to help sustain organizations aligned with his pillars of service, including working to end human trafficking within the human rights arena and promoting human equality, fighting for environment preservation, advocating for the arts and education, and aiding with recovery and assistance.

"My mission is simple: it's to shine a light through music, which can easily be applied to why I sing these songs," Mraz says. "Oftentimes that light is on the very obvious subject of love. This album represents my view of the world and the realization that I am an important part of it in how the choices I make affect other people. But a little bit of love goes a long way, especially on a planet crowded with individuals struggling with seven billion different versions of human triumph and human suffering. When I remember to simply enjoy being where I am, it makes a world of difference."

THE FREEDOM SONG

Words and Music by
Luc Reynaud

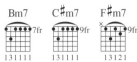

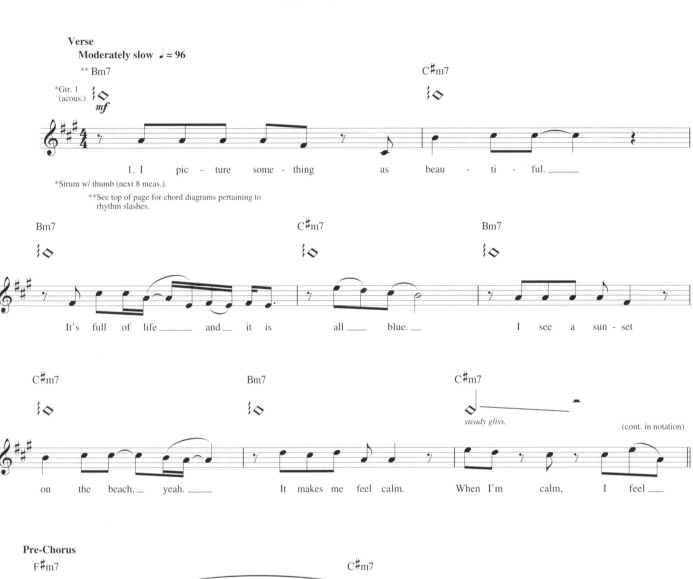

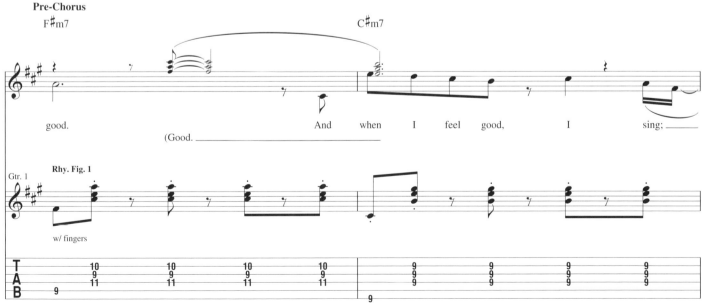

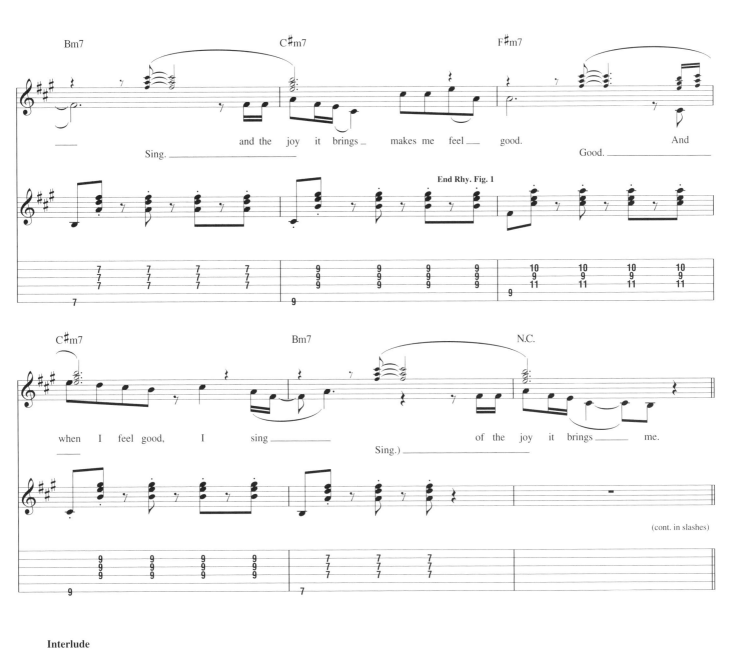

and the joy it brings ___ makes me feel ___ good.
Sing. _____

Good. _____
And

when I feel good, I sing _____
Sing.) _____

of the joy it brings _____ me.

(cont. in slashes)

Interlude

*Strum w/ thumb (next 8 meas.).

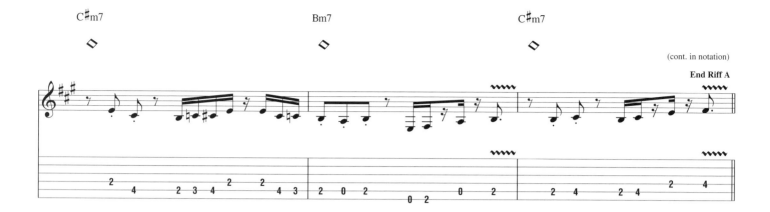

(cont. in notation)

End Riff A

Verse

Gtr. 2 tacet

2. I see birds fly a - cross the sky. _____

(A - cross the

Gtr. 3 (elec.)

mf

w/ clean tone

let ring - - - - - - - - - - - - ┤

*T

*T = Thumb on 6th string

Rhy. Fig. 2

Gtr. 1

w/ fingers

End Rhy. Fig. 2

Gtr. 1: w/ Rhy. Fig. 2 (2 times)

Ev - 'ry - one's heart _____ flies to - geth - er. _____

sky. _____

To - geth - er. _____

Gtr. 3

let ring - - - ┤

T

let ring - - - - - - ┤

T

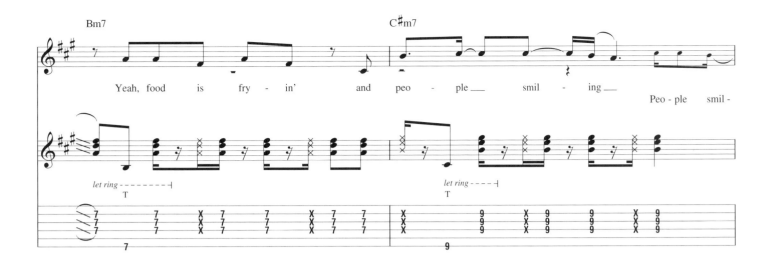

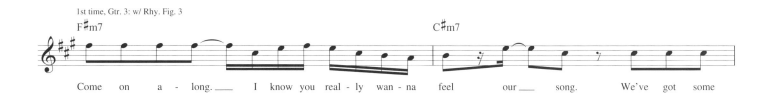

life   to ___ bring.   We've   got   some

To Coda ⊕

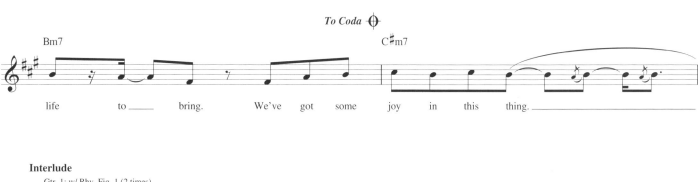

life   to ___ bring.   We've   got   some   joy   in   this   thing. ___

Interlude

Gtr. 1: w/ Rhy. Fig. 1 (2 times)
Gtr. 2: w/ Riff A

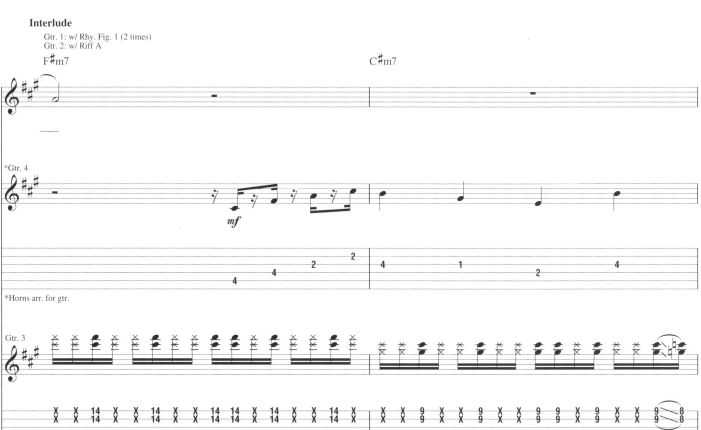

*Horns arr. for gtr.

Outro

Gtr. 1: w/ Rhy. Fig. 1 (4 times)
Gtr. 3: w/ Rhy. Fig. 3 (2 3/4 times)

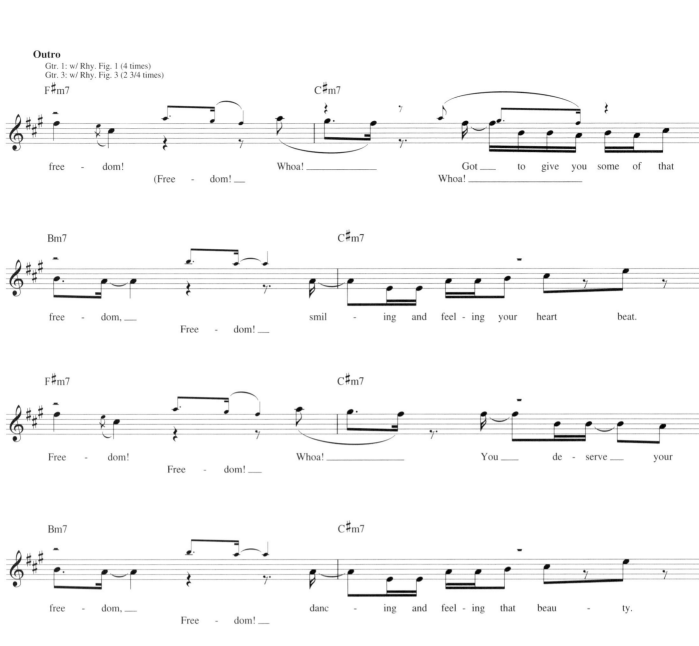

free - dom!

(Free - dom! _____

Whoa! _____

Whoa! _____

Got _____ to give you some of that

free - dom, _____

Free - dom! _____

smil - ing and feel - ing your heart beat.

Free - dom!

Free - dom! _____

Whoa! _____

You _____ de - serve _____ your

free - dom, _____

Free - dom! _____

danc - ing and feel - ing that beau - ty.

Gtr. 2: w/ Riff A

Free - dom!

Free - dom! _____

Whoa! _____

Well, it's

all for you, all for you, all for you, all for you. Sing,

All for you, all for you, all for you. Oh! _____

Gtr. 3

```
12 12 X X 14 14 X X 17 17 X X 17 17     17
12 12 X X 14 14 X X 17 17 X X 17 17     17
```

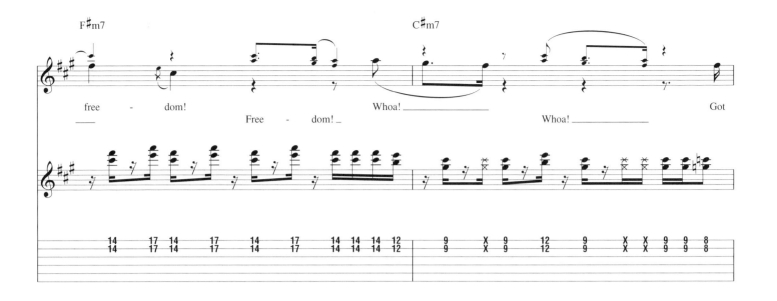

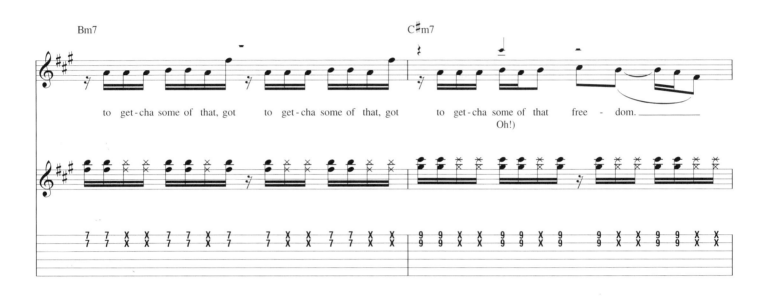

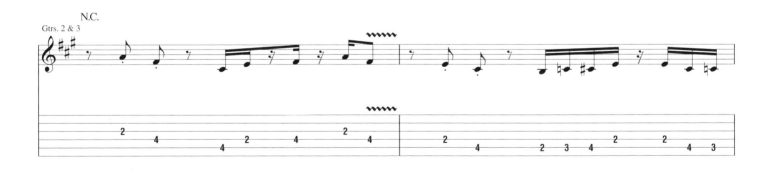

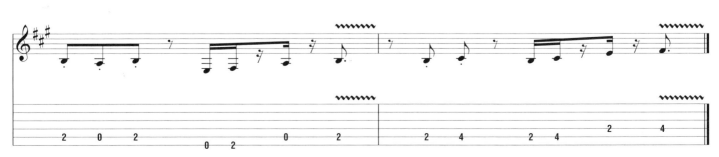

LIVING IN THE MOMENT

Words and Music by
Jason Mraz and Rick Nowels

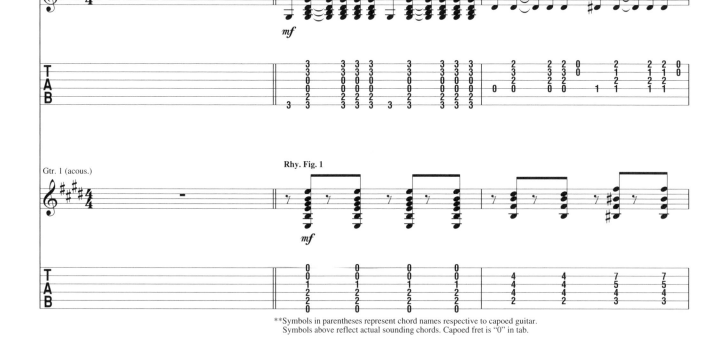

Whistle…

**Symbols in parentheses represent chord names respective to capoed guitar.
Symbols above reflect actual sounding chords. Capoed fret is "0" in tab.

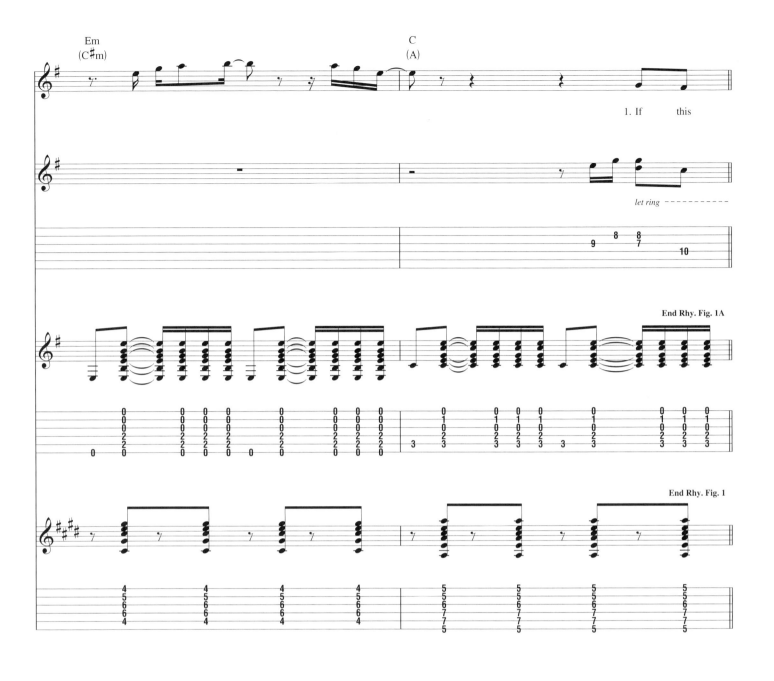

Verse
Gtrs. 1 & 2: w/ Rhy. Figs. 1 & 1A (2 times)

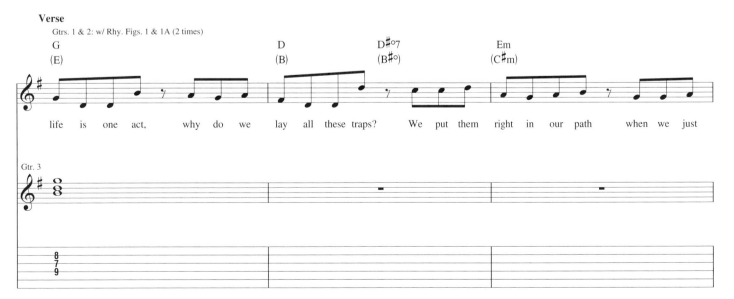

life is one act, why do we lay all these traps? We put them right in our path when we just

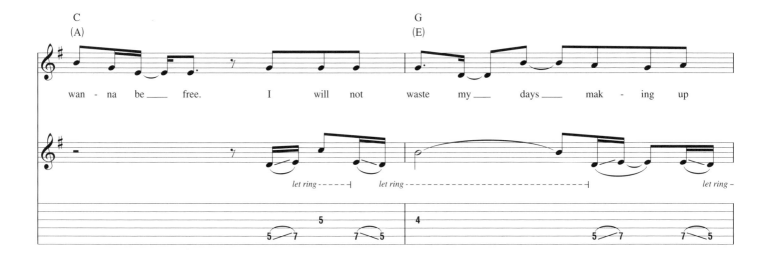

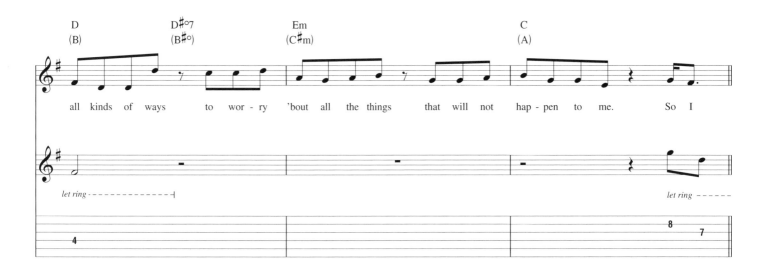

Pre-Chorus

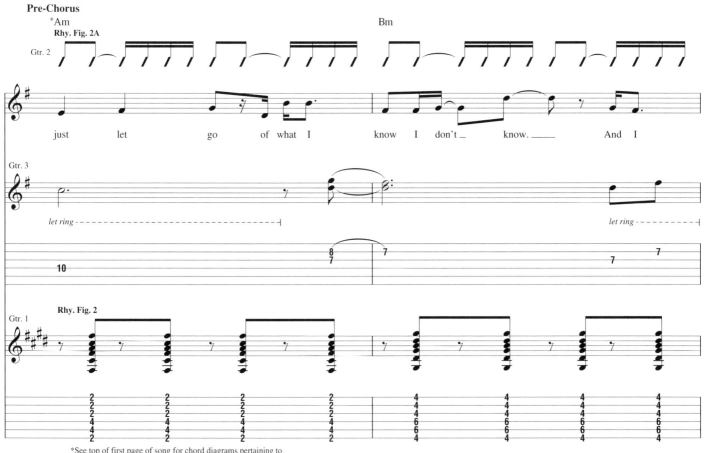

*See top of first page of song for chord diagrams pertaining to rhythm slashes.

16

know I on-ly _____ do this by _____ liv-ing in the

Chorus
Gtrs. 1 & 2: w/ Rhy. Figs. 1 & 1A (2 times)
Gtr. 3 tacet

mo-ment, _____ liv-ing my life, _____ eas-y and _____

Riff A
Gtr. 4 (elec.)

breez - y with peace _____ in my mind, with peace _____ in my

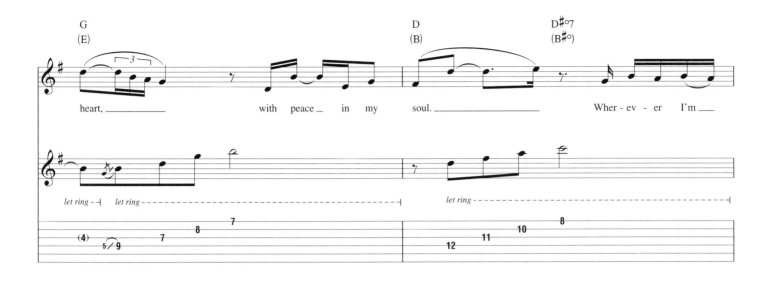

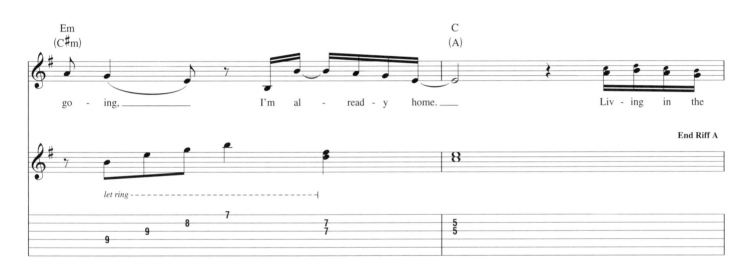

Bridge

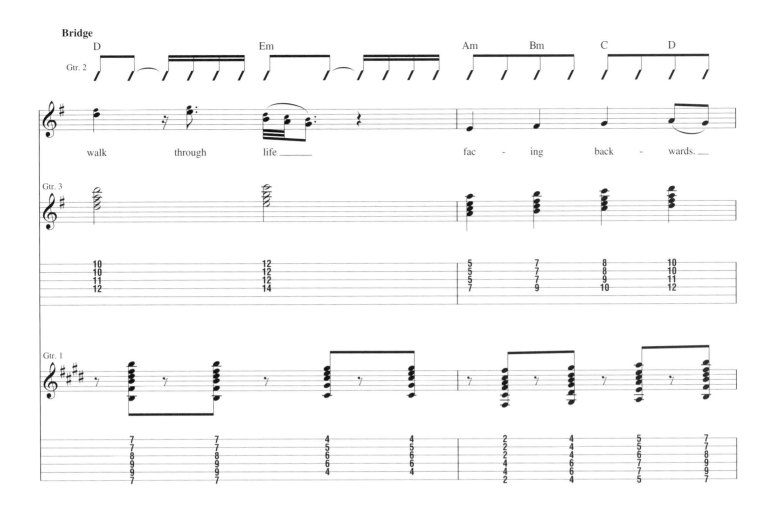

walk   through   life _____   fac - ing   back - wards. __

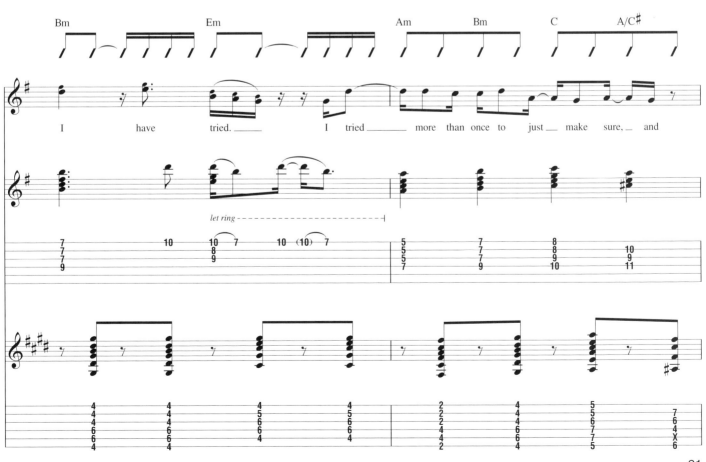

I   have   tried. _____   I   tried _____   more than once to just __ make   sure, __   and

Chorus
Gtrs. 1 & 2: w/ Rhy. Figs. 1 & 1A (2 times)
Gtr. 4: w/ Riff A
Gtr. 5 tacet

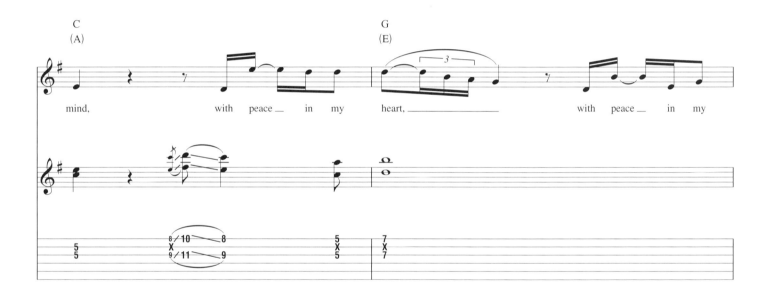

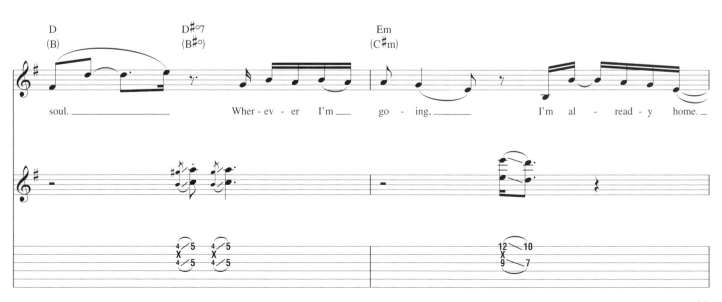

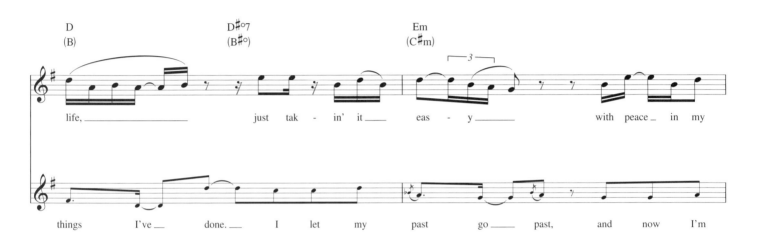

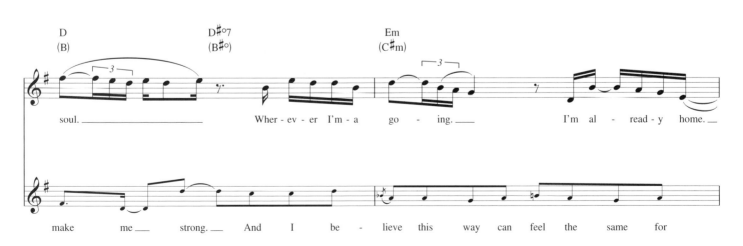

THE WOMAN I LOVE

Words and Music by
Jason Mraz and David Hodges

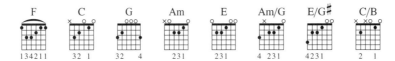

Capo IV

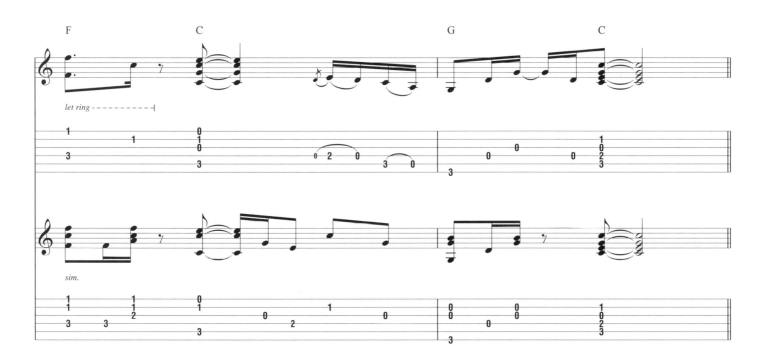

Verse

Gtr. 2 tacet

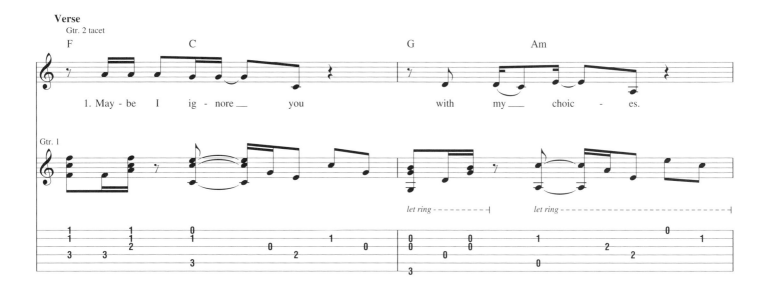

1. May - be I ig - nore ___ you with my ___ choic - es.

Gtr. 1

let ring ---------- let ring ------------------------

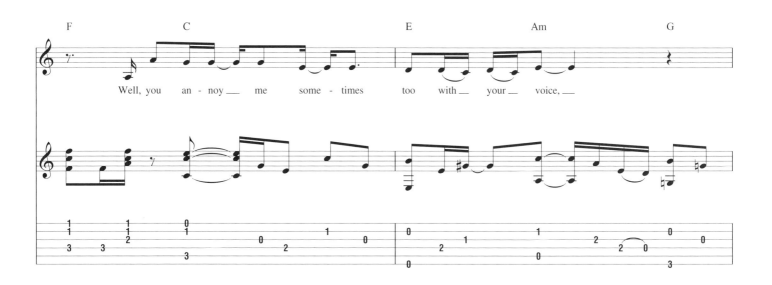

Well, you an - noy ___ me some - times too with ___ your ___ voice, ___

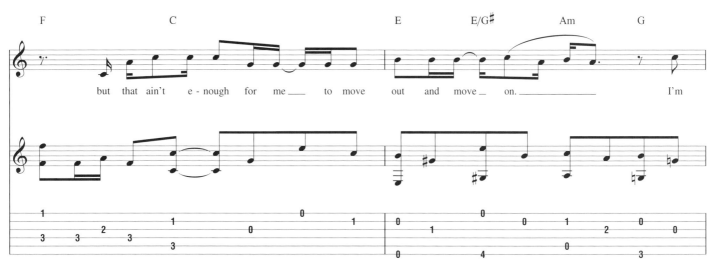

but that ain't e - nough for me ___ to move out and move ___ on. _____ I'm

*Set for eighth note regeneration w/ 1 repeat.

(cont. in slashes)

Verse

Gtr. 2 tacet

2. We don't have to hur - ry and you can take as long_ as you want._

*Strum w/ fingers.

**See top of first page of song for chord diagrams pertaining to
    rhythm slashes.

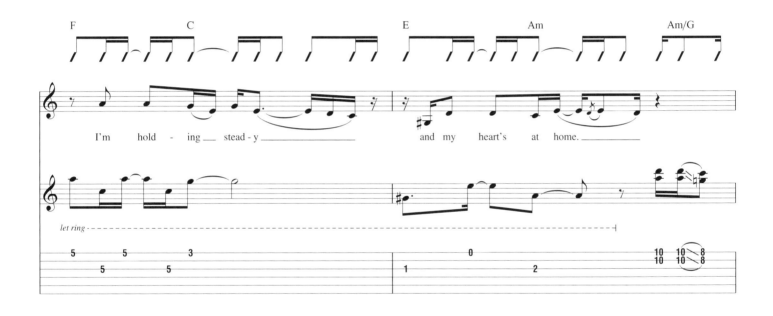

I'm hold - ing_ stead - y _____ and my heart's at home. _____

With my hand be - hind_ you, I will catch you if ___ you fall. _____ I'm

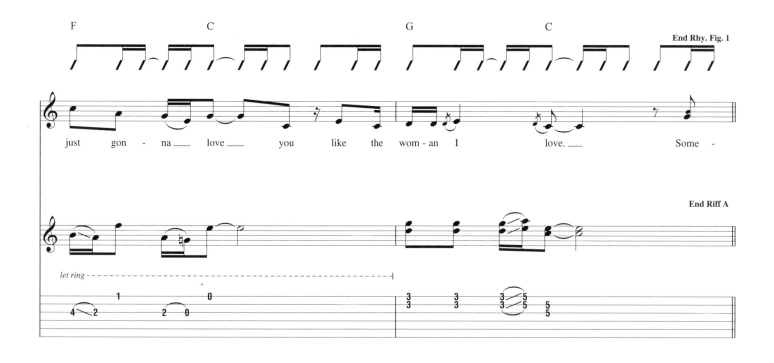

just gon - na ___ love ___ you like the wom - an I love. ___ Some -

Bridge

Gtr. 3 tacet

times the world can make _ you feel you're not wel - come an - y - more. ___ And you

*Two gtrs. arr. for one

beat your-self __ up; you let your-self __ get __ mad. _____ And in those

times when you stop lov-ing the wom-an I a-dore, _____ you can re-

lax, __ be-cause, babe, I got __ your back. _____ Mm, I got __

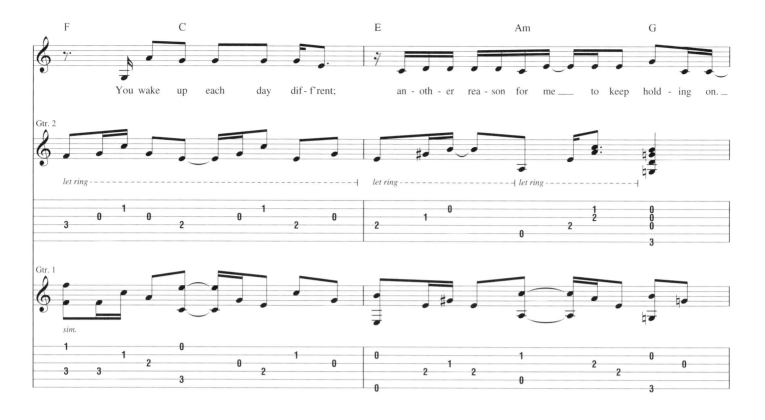

You wake up each day dif-f'rent; an-oth-er rea-son for me ___ to keep hold-ing on. ___

___ I'm not at-tached to an-y way you're show-ing up. ___ I'm

just gon - na ___ love ___ you like the wom-an I love. ___ Yeah,

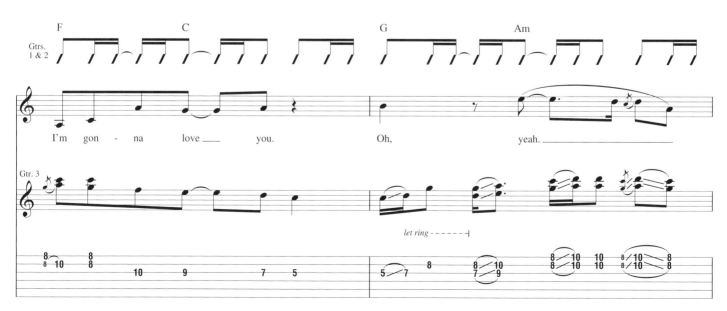

I'm gon - na love ___ you. Oh, yeah. ___

I'm gon - na love you. You're the wom - an I love.

Outro

Gtrs. 1 & 2: w/ Rhy. Fig. 1 (1st 6 meas.)
Gtr. 5: w/ Riff B

I WON'T GIVE UP

Words and Music by
Jason Mraz and Michael Natter

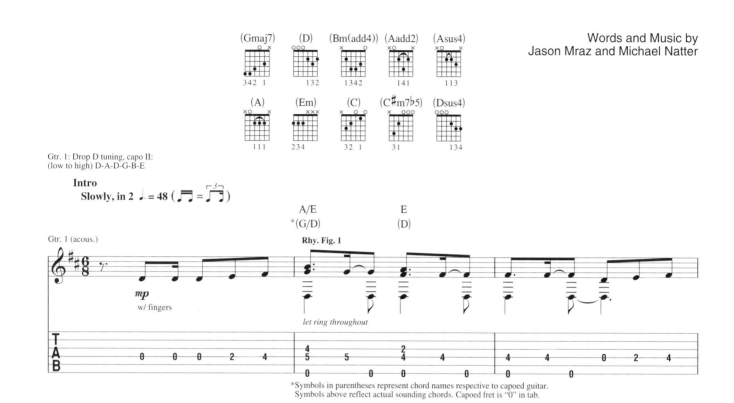

*Symbols in parentheses represent chord names respective to capoed guitar.
Symbols above reflect actual sounding chords. Capoed fret is "0" in tab.

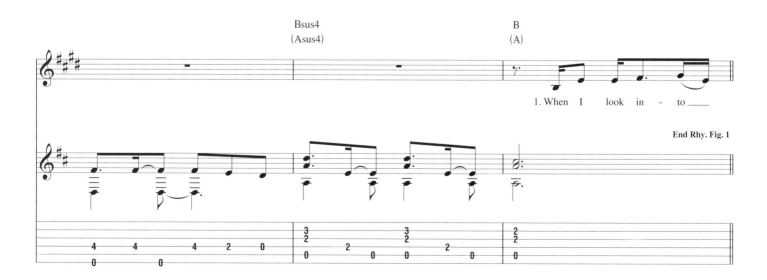

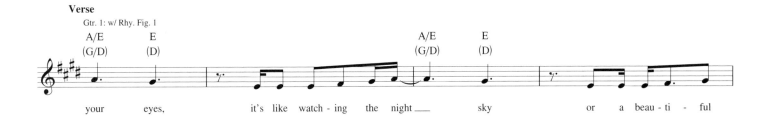

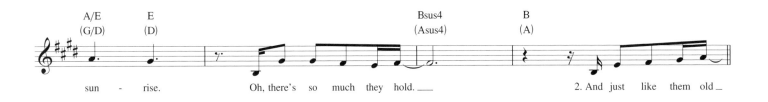

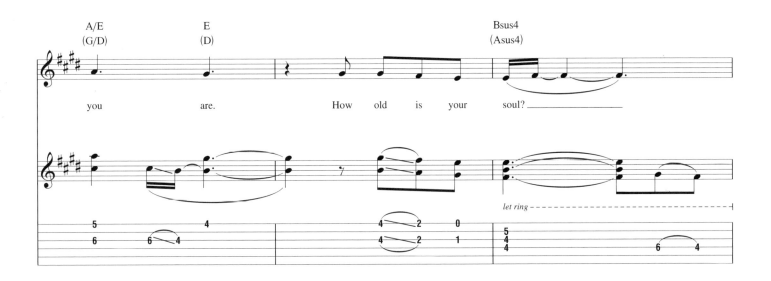

Chorus

Well, I won't give up ____ on us ____ e - ven if the

skies ____ get ____ rough. ____ I'm giv - ing ____ you all _____ my

Chorus

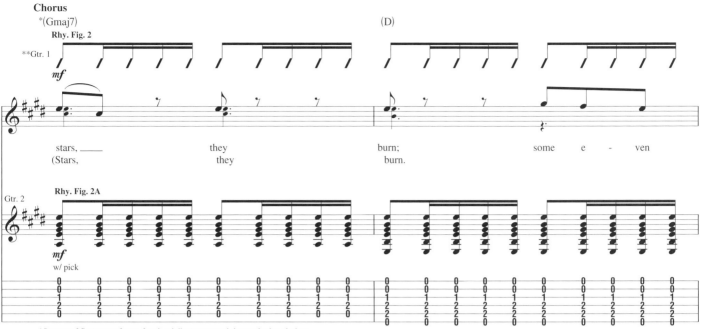

*See top of first page of song for chord diagrams pertaining to rhythm slashes.
**w/ pick

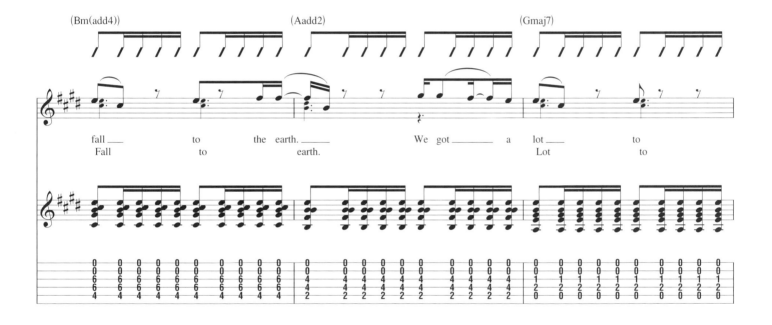

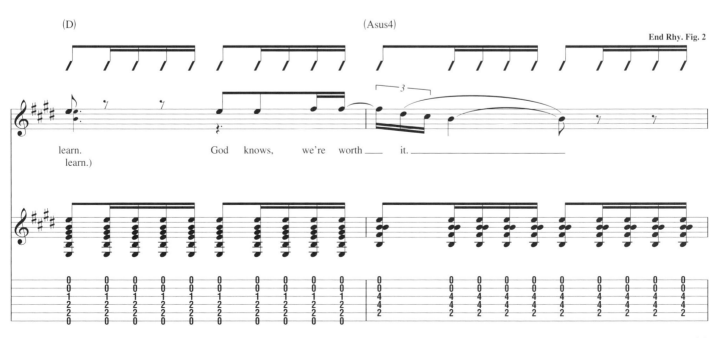

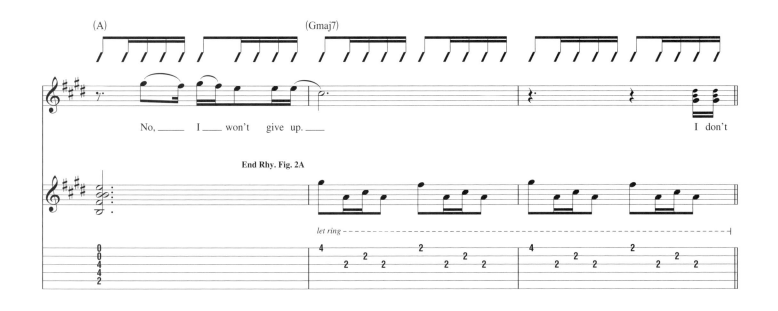

No,____ I ____ won't give up.____ I don't

Bridge

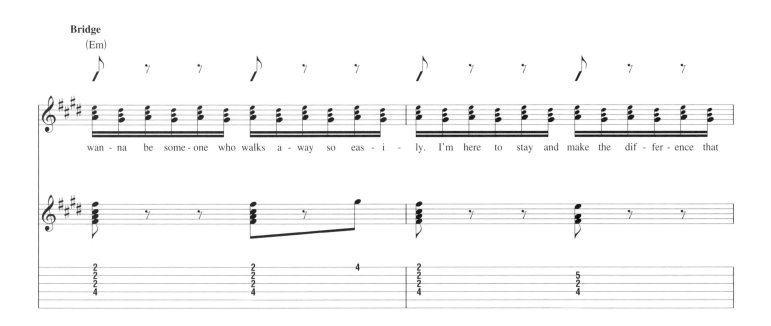

wan-na be some-one who walks a-way so eas-i-ly. I'm here to stay and make the dif-fer-ence that

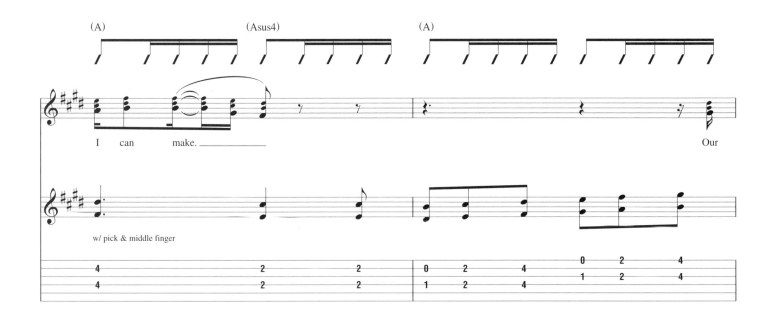

I can make._____ Our

w/ pick & middle finger

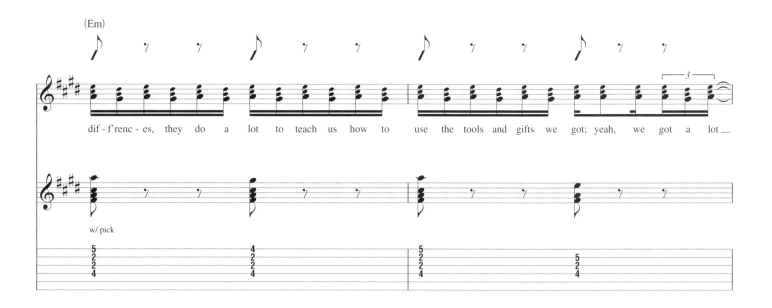

dif - f'renc - es, they do a lot to teach us how to use the tools and gifts we got; yeah, we got a lot __

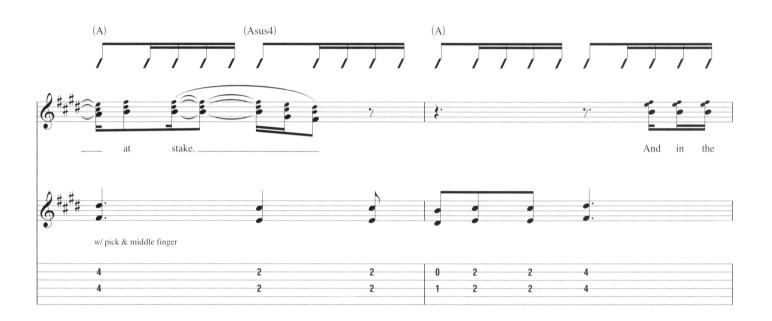

__ at stake. __ And in the

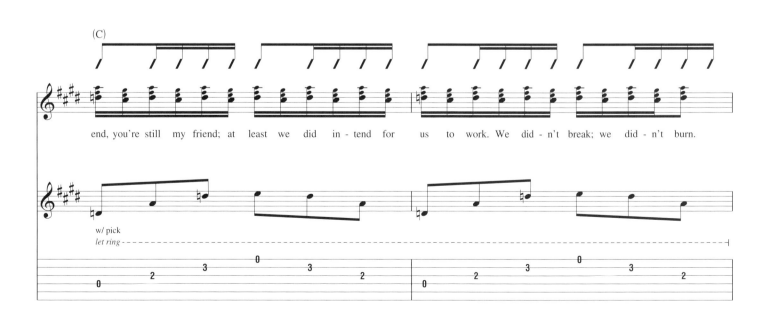

end, you're still my friend; at least we did in - tend for us to work. We did - n't break; we did - n't burn.

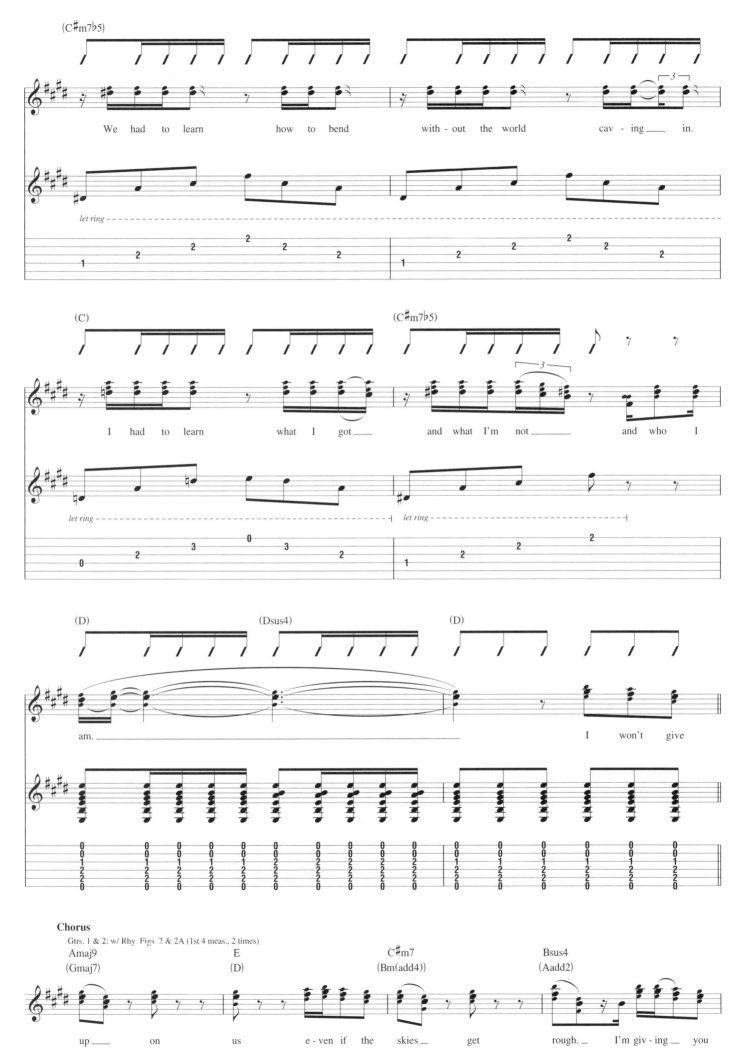

5/6

Words and Music by
Jason Mraz and Michael Natter

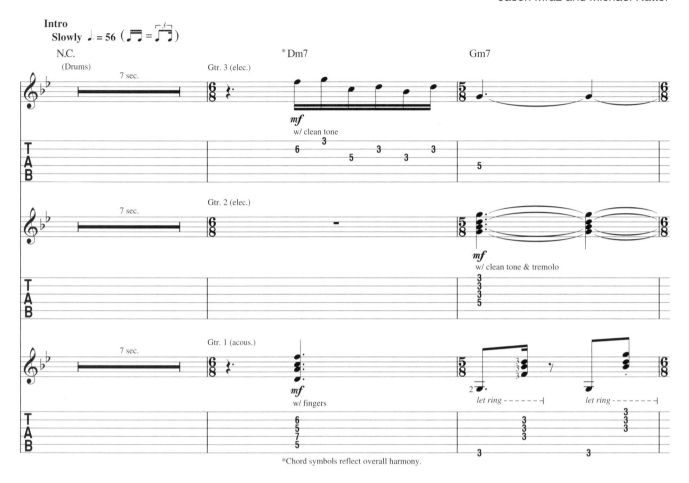

*Chord symbols reflect overall harmony.

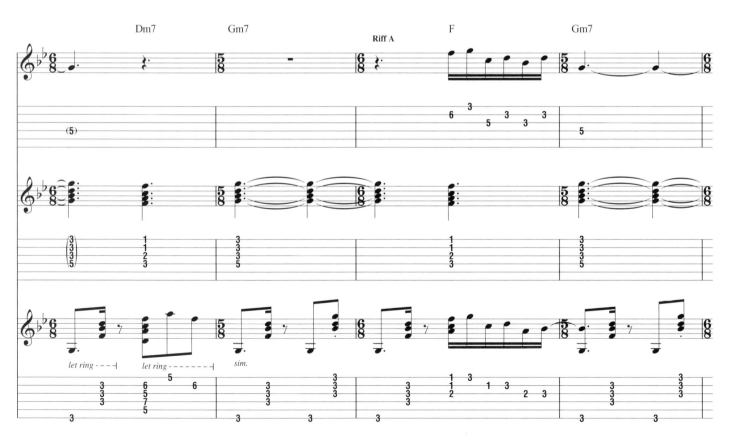

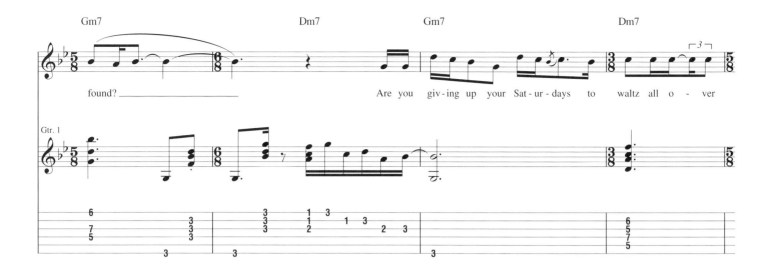

found? _____

Are you giv-ing up your Sat-ur-days to waltz all o-ver

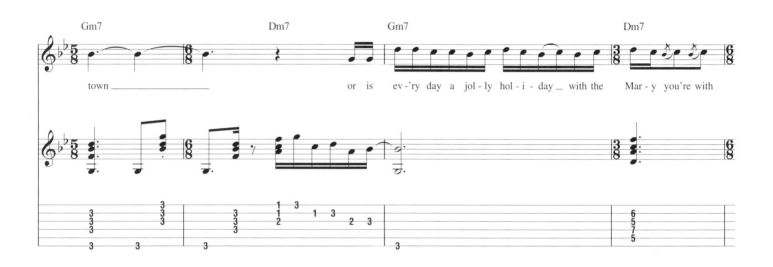

town _____

or is ev-'ry day a jol-ly hol-i-day _ with the Mar-y you're with

⑃ Chorus

3rd time, Gtr. 4 tacet

now? _____

You could give it all _____ a-way, give it

all ____ and be un-stop-pa - ble. _____ All ____ a - way. ____ { 1., 3. Ev -'ry-thing is real - ly pos-si - ble. _____ }
{ 2. M-m-m-make emp - ty mean - ing - ful. }

To Coda 1 ⊕
To Coda 2 ⊕

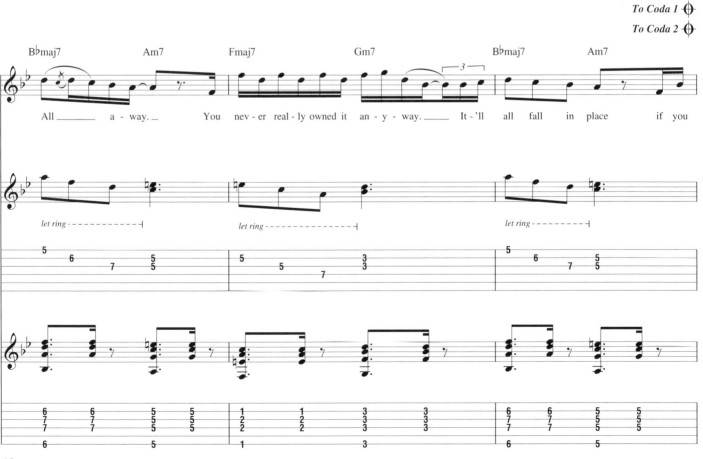

All ____ a - way. ____ You nev - er real - ly owned it an - y - way. ___ It -'ll all fall in place if you

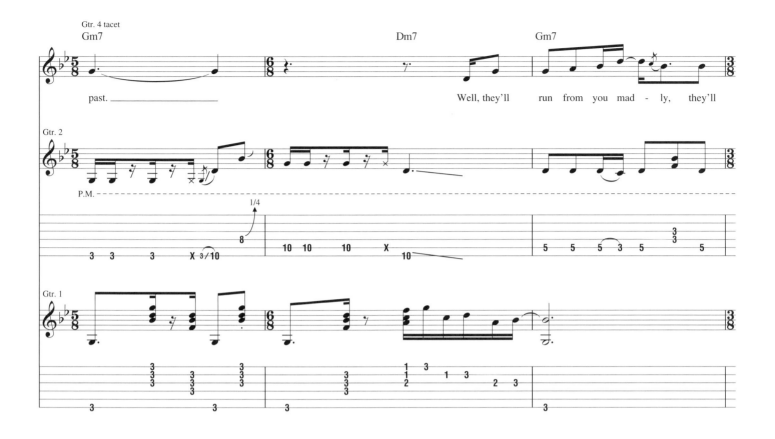

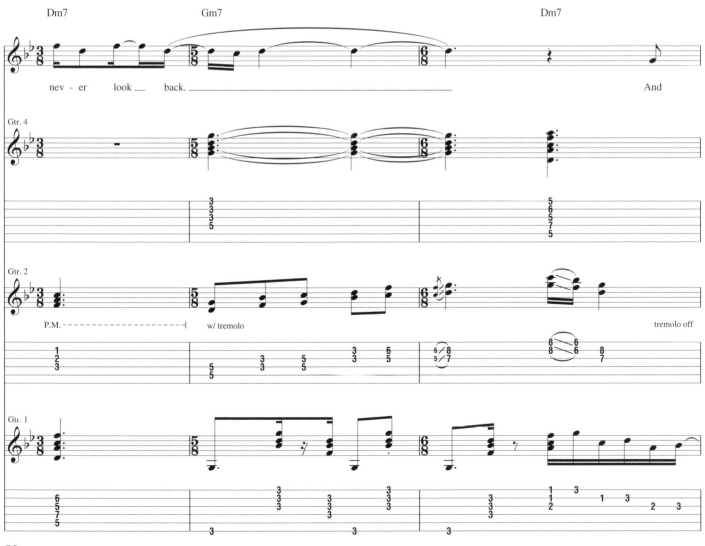

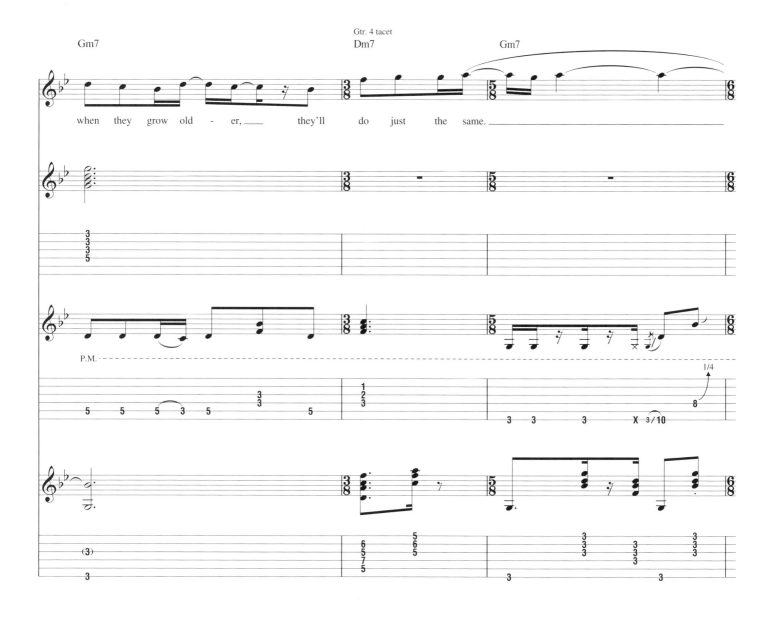

when they grow old - er, ___ they'll do just the same. ___

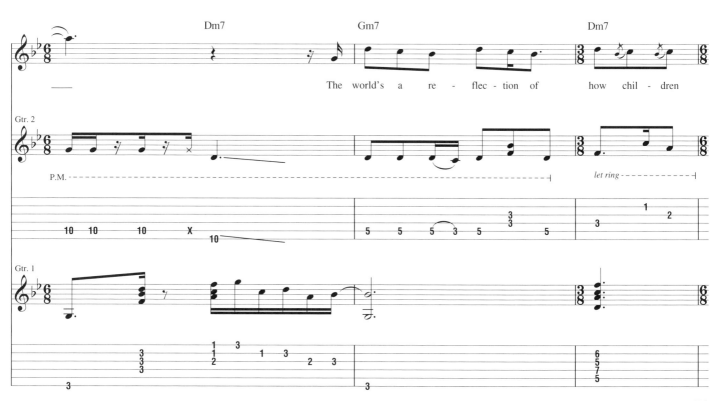

The world's a re - flec - tion of how chil - dren

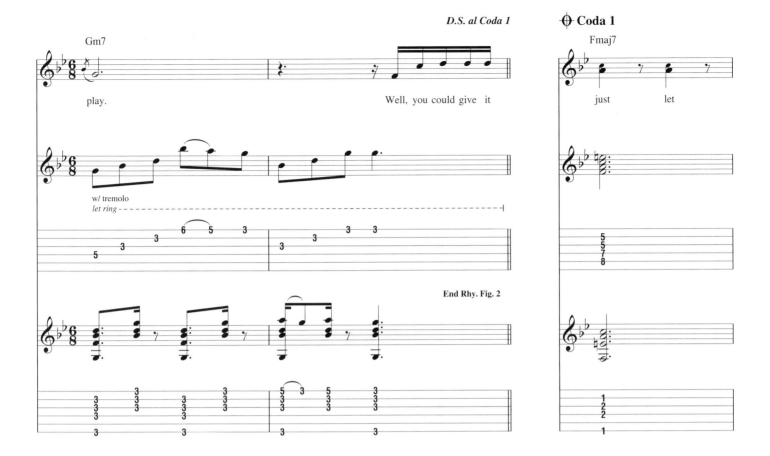

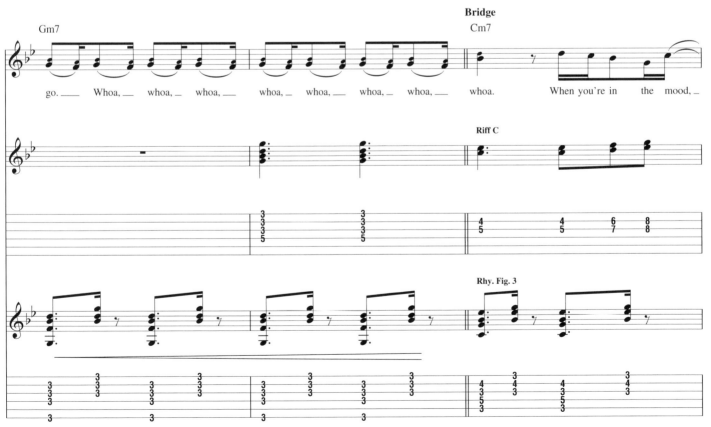

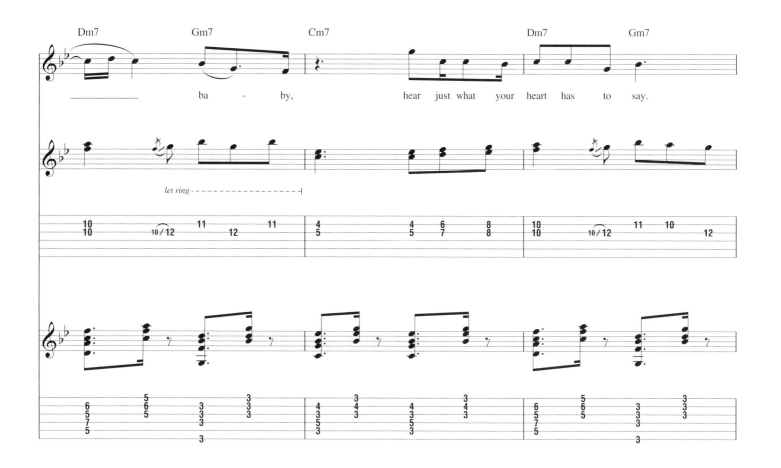

ba - by,   hear just what your heart has to say.

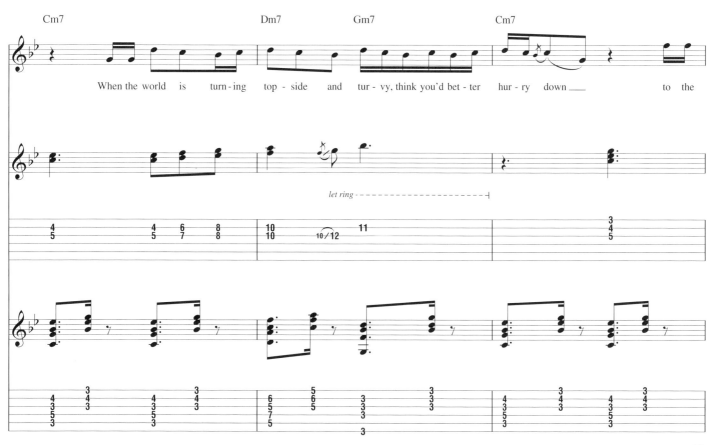

When the world is turn - ing top - side and tur - vy, think you'd bet - ter hur - ry down __ to the

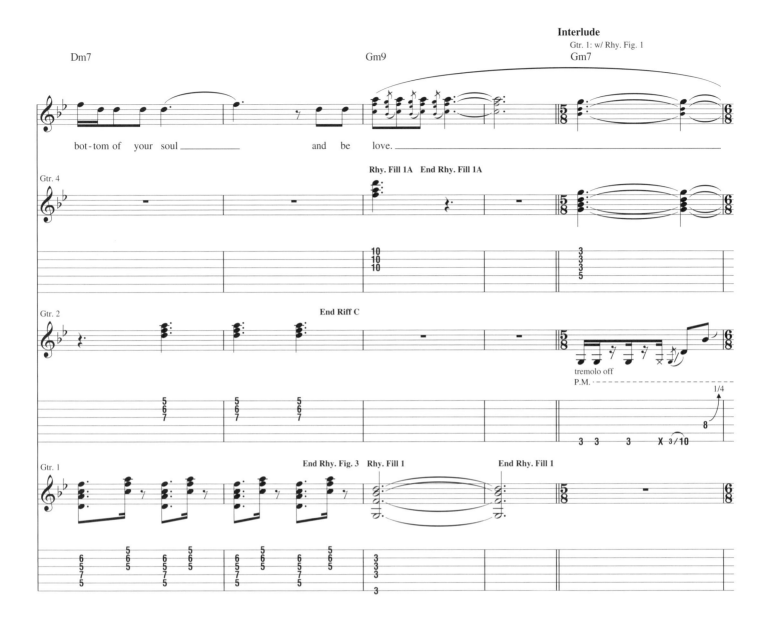

bot-tom of your soul _____ and be love. _____

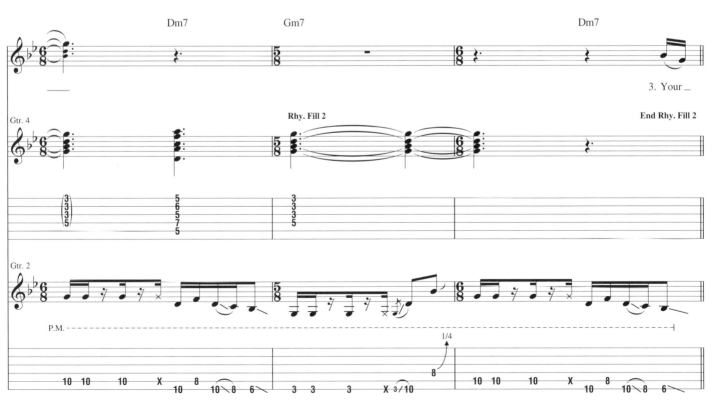

3. Your _

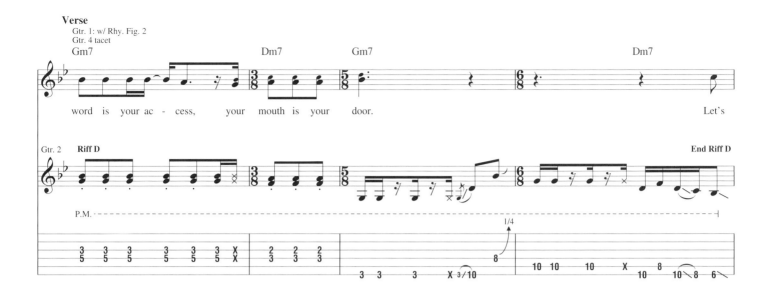

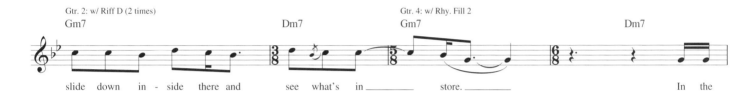

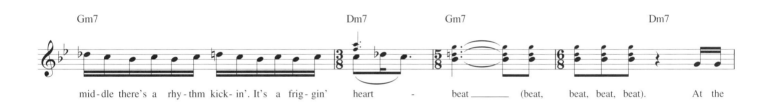

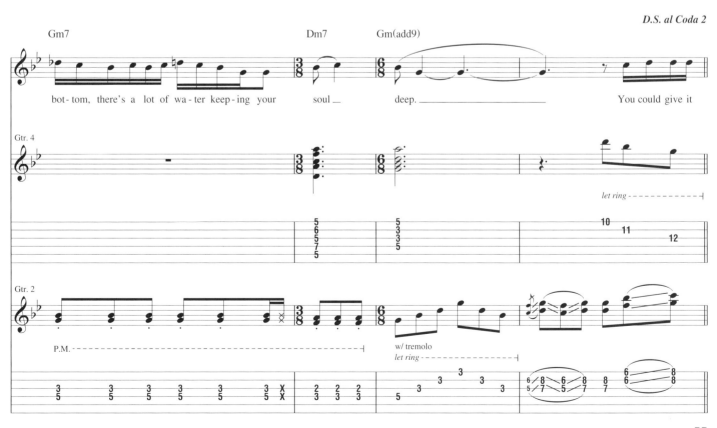

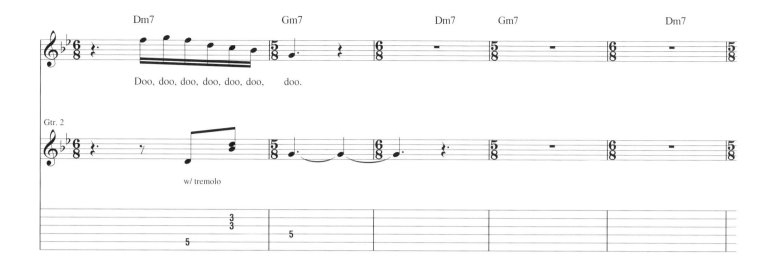

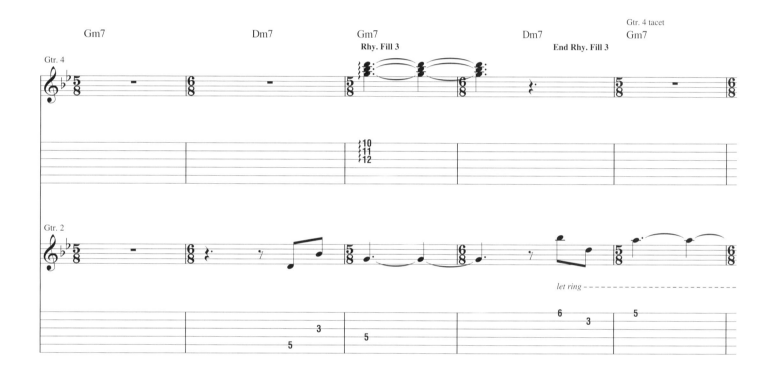

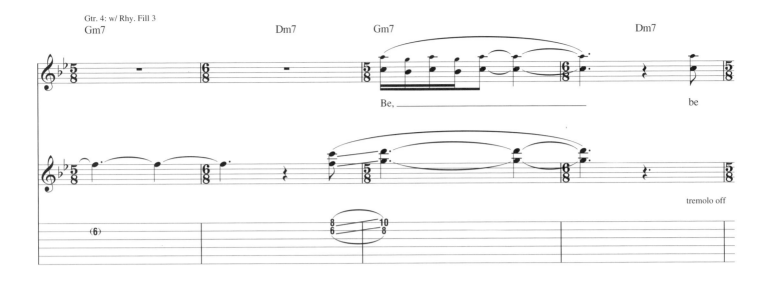

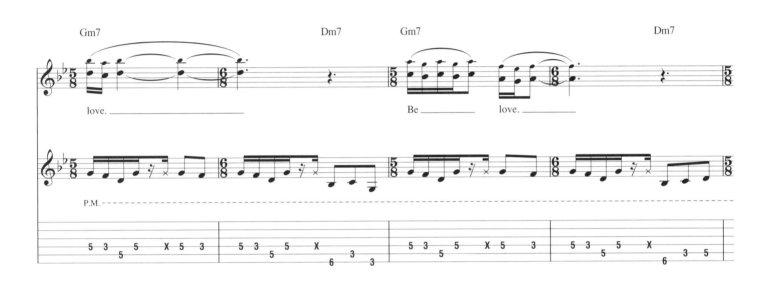

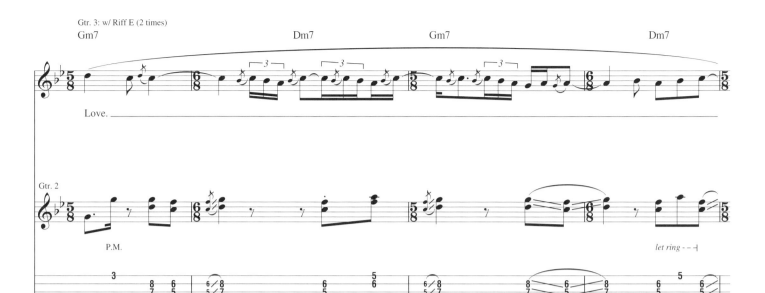

EVERYTHING IS SOUND (LA LA LA)

Words and Music by
Jason Mraz, Matt Hales,
Mike Daly and Martin Terefe

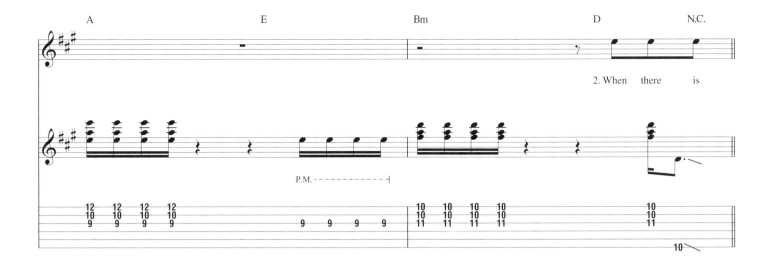

Verse

Gtr. 1: w/ Rhy. Fig. 1 (4 times)
Gtr. 2 tacet

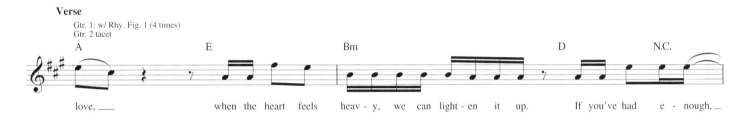

love, ___ when the heart feels heav-y, we can light-en it up. If you've had e-nough, ___

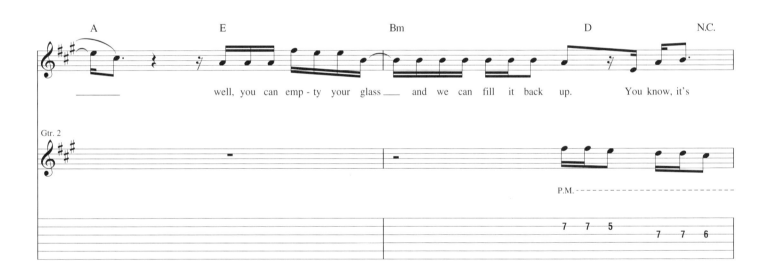

___ well, you can emp-ty your glass ___ and we can fill it back up. You know, it's

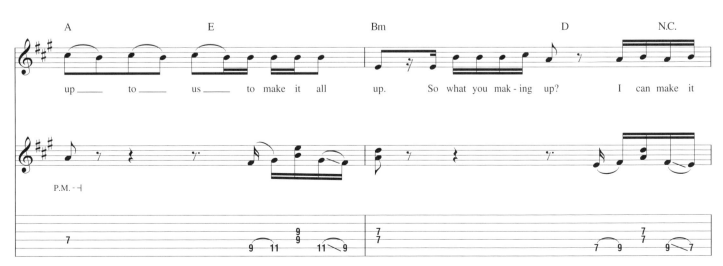

up ___ to ___ us ___ to make it all up. So what you mak-ing up? I can make it

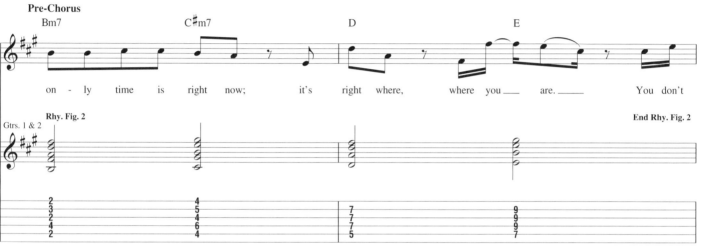

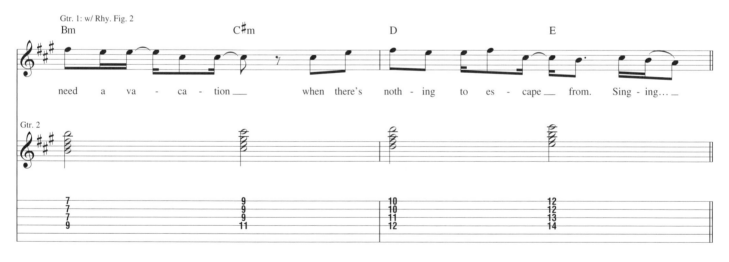

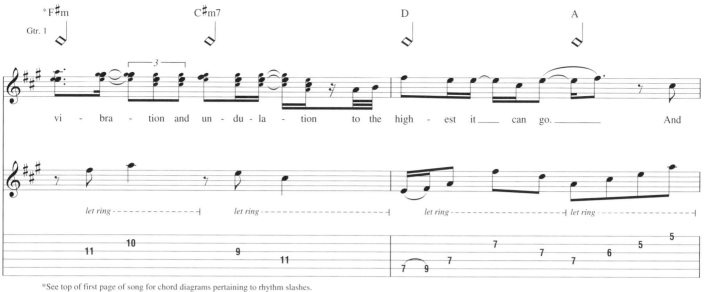

vi - bra - tion and un - du - la - tion to the high - est it __ can go. _____ And

*See top of first page of song for chord diagrams pertaining to rhythm slashes.

trust me, hear me. If it makes you wan - na sing, ___ just sing it...

§ **Chorus**

Chorus

1st time, Gtr. 1: w/ Rhy. Fig. 1 (4 times)
1st time, Gtr. 2: w/ Rhy. Fig. 3 (2 times)
2nd time, Gtr. 1: w/ Rhy. Fig. 1 (8 times)
2nd time, Gtr. 2: w/ Rhy. Fig. 3 (4 times)

Ha, la, la, la, la, ___ la, la, ___ yeah.   Ha, la, la, la, la, ___ la, let's all

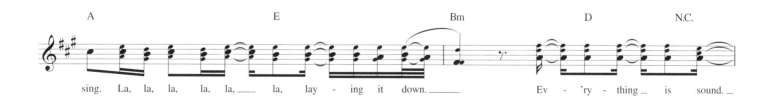

sing. La, la, la, la, la, ___ la, lay - ing it down. ___   Ev - 'ry - thing __ is sound. __

___ Ha - le - la - la - la - la, ___ yeah.   Ha - le - la - la - la, let's all

Ha - le - la - la - la - la - la - la, yeah. Ha - le - la - la - la - la, let's all

sing. Ha - le - la - la - la - la - le - lu - jah.

Ha - le - la - la - la - la - la, ___ yeah. Ha - le - la - la - la - la, ___ let's ___ all ___

(Ha - le - la - la - la - la - la - la. Ha - le - la - la - la - la.

sing. Ha - le - la - la - la - la - le - lu - jah.

Ha - le - la - la - la - la - le - lu - jah.

Ha - le - la - la - la - la - la, yeah. Ha - le - la - la - la - la - le - lu -

Ha - le - la - la - la - la - la. Ha - le - la - la - la - la.

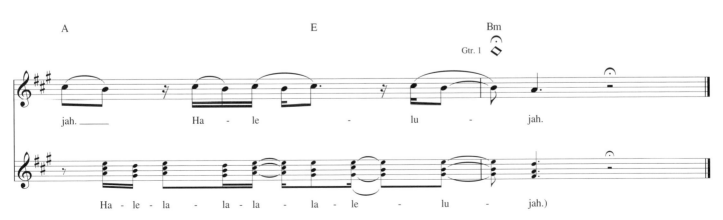

jah. ___ Ha - le - lu - jah.

Ha - le - la - la - la - la - le - lu - jah.)

93 MILLION MILES

*All music sounds 1/2 step higher than indicated due to capo. Capoed fret is "0" in tab.

(cont. in slashes)

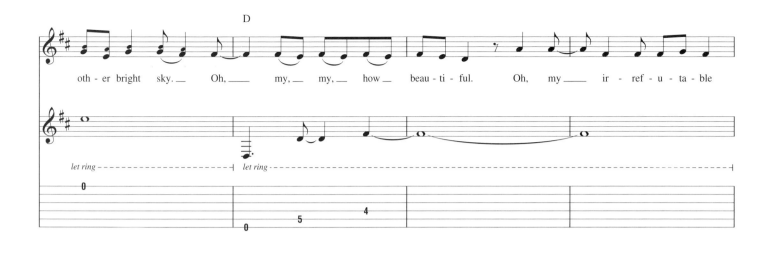

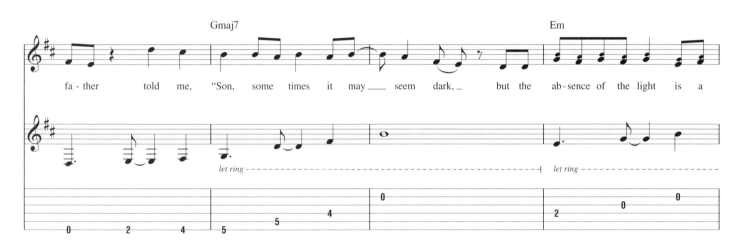

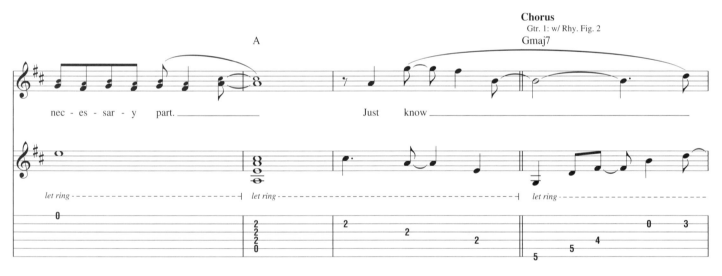

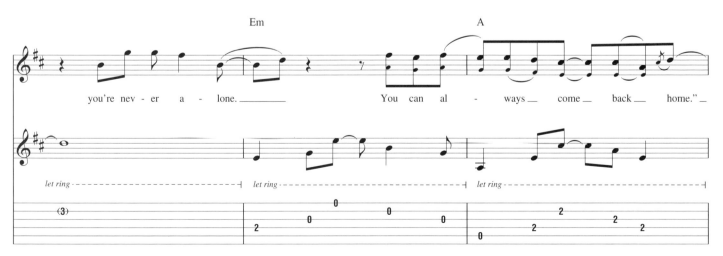

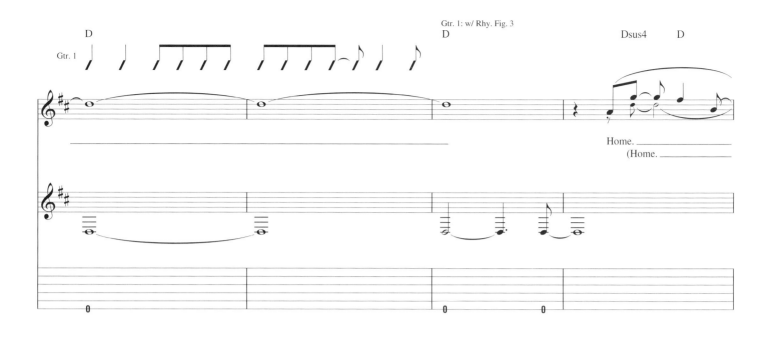

Half-time feel

End half-time feel

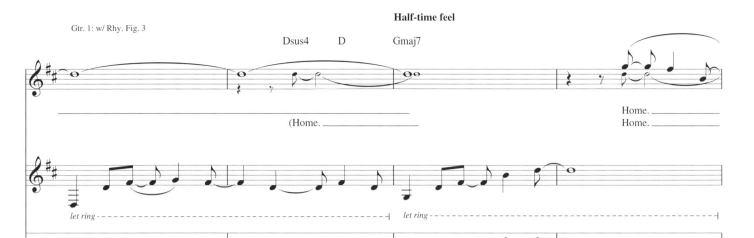

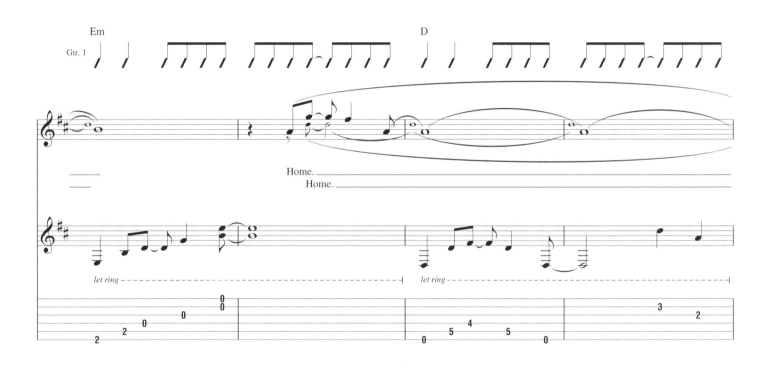

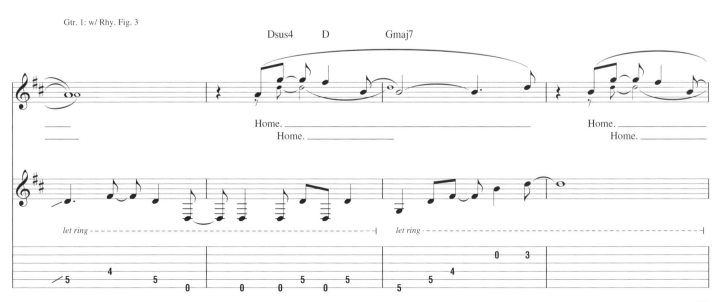

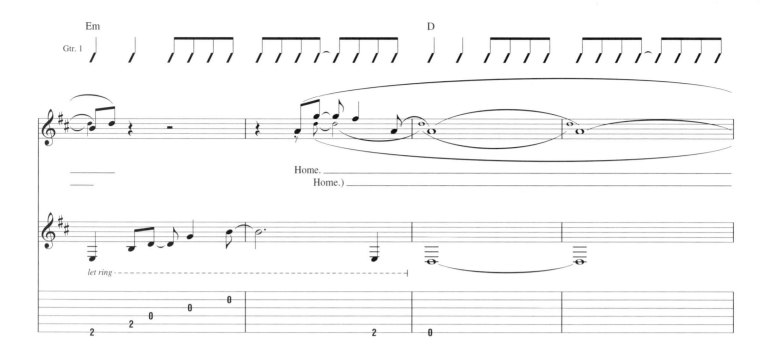

Outro-Verse

End half-time feel

Gtr. 1: w/ Rhy. Fig. 1 (1st 8 meas.)

3. Nine - ty - three mil - lion miles __ from the sun.

Gtr. 2 tacet

Peo - ple, get read - y, get read - y 'cause here it comes. It's a light, a beau - ti - ful light, __ o -

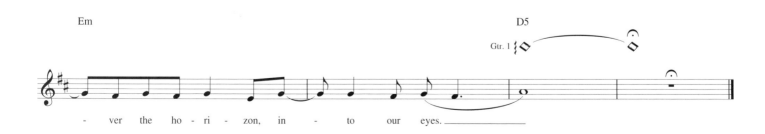

- ver the ho - ri - zon, in - to our eyes. _____

FRANK D. FIXER

Words and Music by
Jason Mraz, Martin Terefe
and Sacha Skarbek

Pre-Chorus

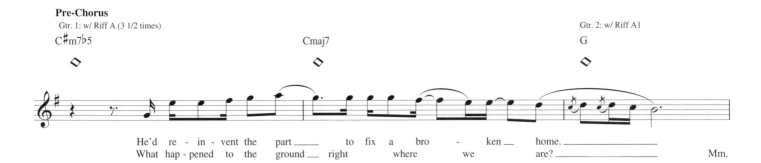

Gtr. 1: w/ Riff A (3 1/2 times)
Gtr. 2: w/ Riff A1

C#m7♭5 · Cmaj7 · G

He'd re-in-vent the part ___ to fix a bro-ken ___ home. ___
What hap-pened to the ground ___ right where we are? ___ Mm.

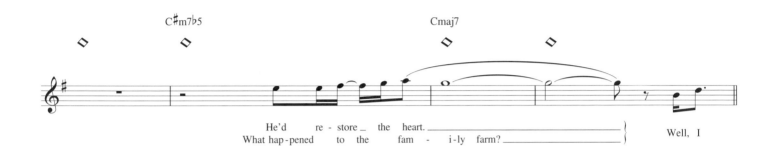

C#m7♭5 · Cmaj7

He'd re-store _ the heart. ___
What hap-pened to the fam-i-ly farm? ___ Well, I

Chorus

Gtr. 3 tacet

C^type2 · Dadd4 · G · C^type2 · Dadd4

Rhy. Fig. 1A
Gtr. 4 (acous.) *mp*

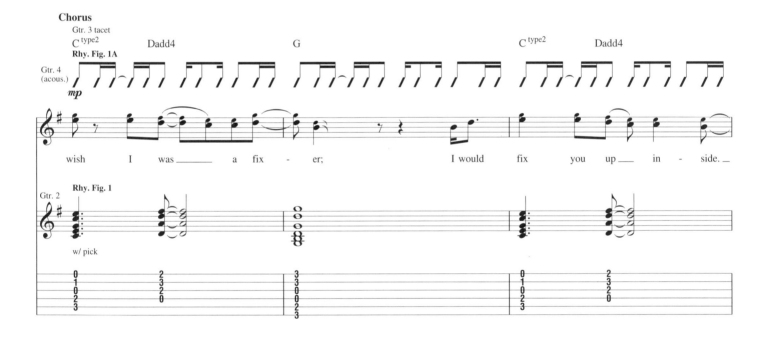

wish I was ___ a fix-er; I would fix you up ___ in-side. ___

Rhy. Fig. 1
Gtr. 2
w/ pick

Em(add2) · C^type2 · Dadd4 · G · A7

End Rhy. Fig. 1A

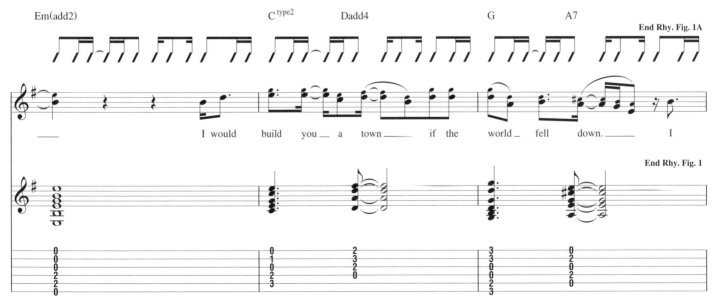

___ I would build you _ a town ___ if the world _ fell down. ___ I

End Rhy. Fig. 1

Bridge

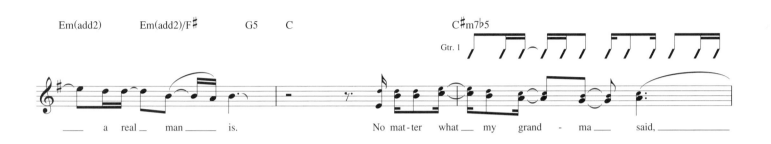

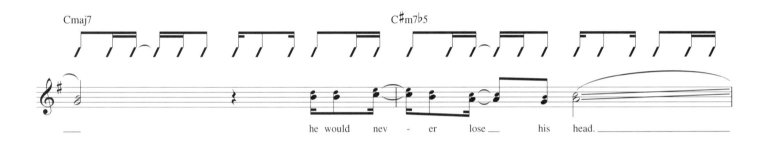

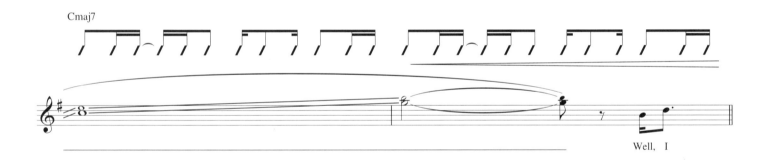

Chorus

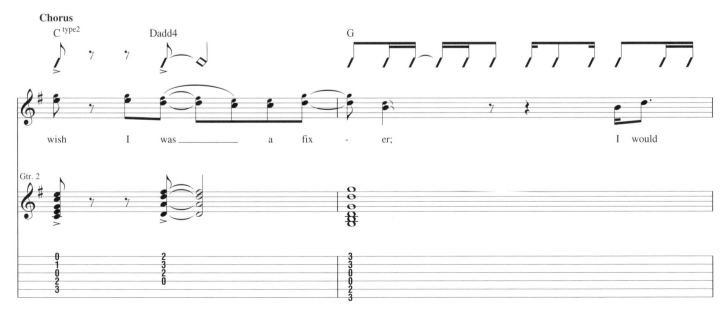

fix you up ____ in - side. _____ I would

build you ____ a town _____ if the world ___ fell down. _____ I

wish ___ I was _____ that guy. _____ Well, I

Rhy. Fig. 3

End Rhy. Fig. 3

Gtrs. 1 & 2: w/ Rhy. Figs. 1 & 1A

wish I was _____ a farm - er; I would grow you a Gar - den of ___ E -

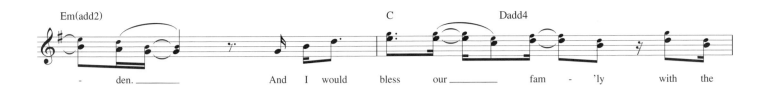

- den. _____ And I would bless our _____ fam - 'ly with the

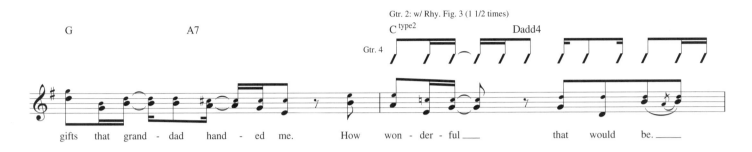

gifts that grand - dad hand - ed me. How won - der - ful _____ that would be. _____

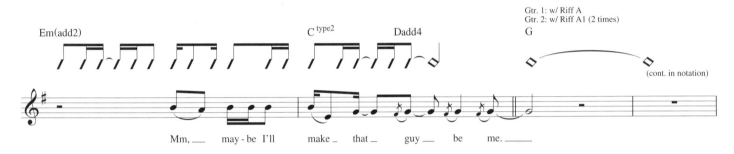

Mm, _____ may - be I'll make _ that _ guy _ be me. _____

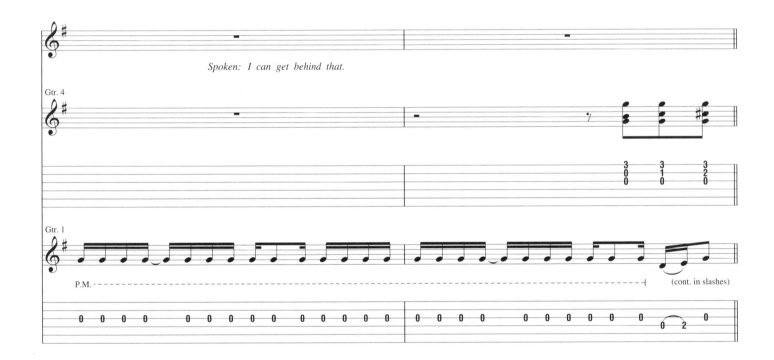

Spoken: I can get behind that.

Outro-Harmonica Solo

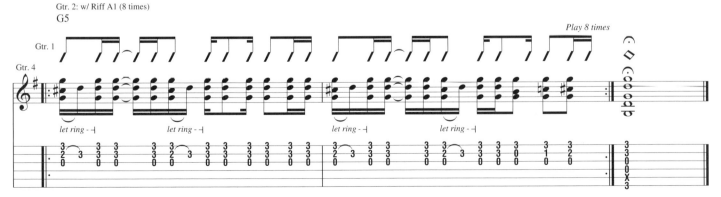

WHO'S THINKING ABOUT YOU NOW?

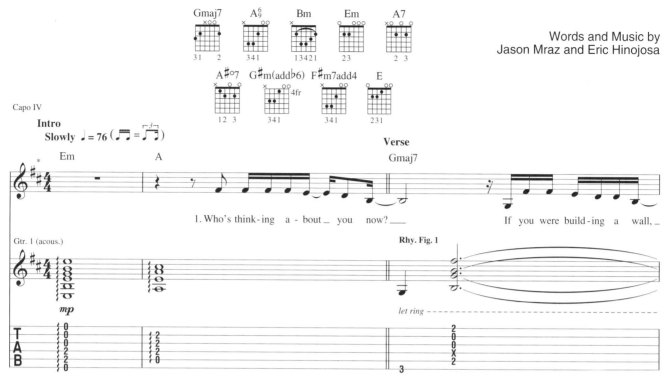

Words and Music by
Jason Mraz and Eric Hinojosa

*All music sounds a major 3rd higher than indicated due to capo. Capoed fret is "0" in tab.

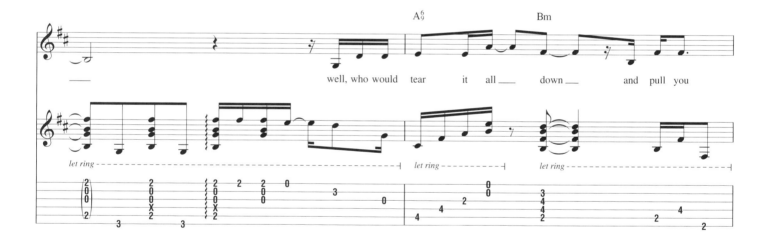

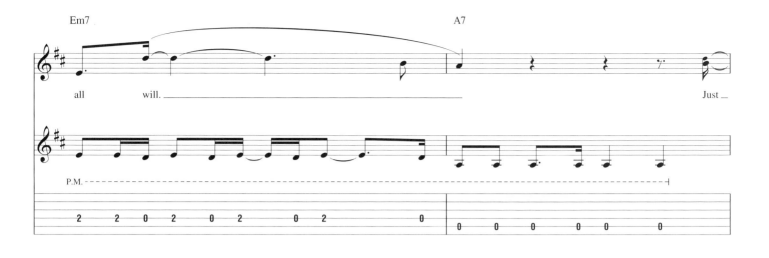

all will. _____ Just _

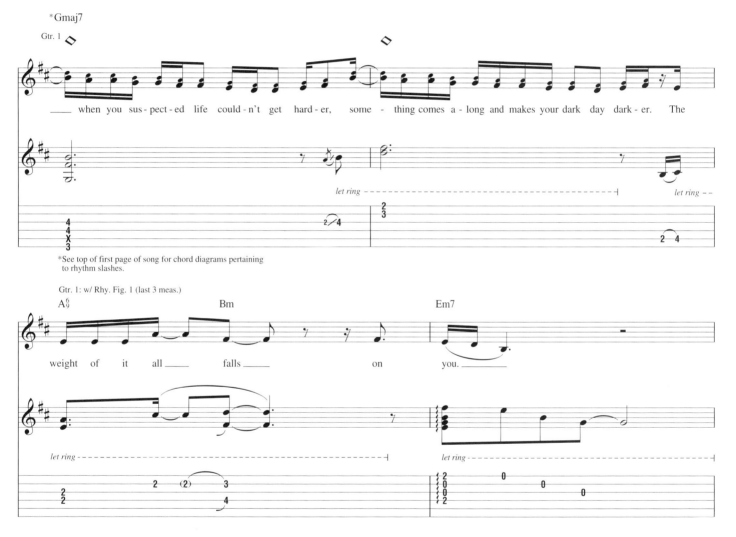

*Gmaj7

____ when you sus-pect-ed life could-n't get hard-er, some-thing comes a-long and makes your dark day dark-er. The

*See top of first page of song for chord diagrams pertaining to rhythm slashes.

Gtr. 1: w/ Rhy. Fig. 1 (last 3 meas.)

A⁶/₉   Bm   Em7

weight of it all ____ falls ____ on   you. ____

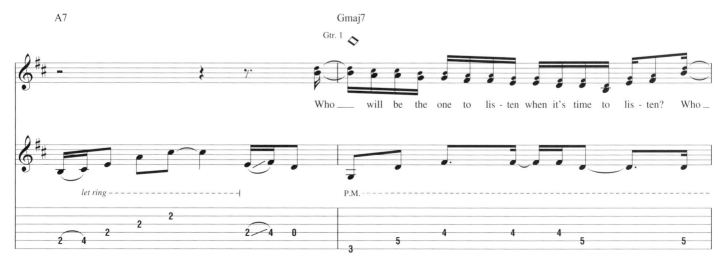

A7   Gmaj7

Who ____ will be the one to lis-ten when it's time to lis-ten? Who _

Verse

-ing some-thing. I feel like call - ing off __ the day __ to be with

you. _____

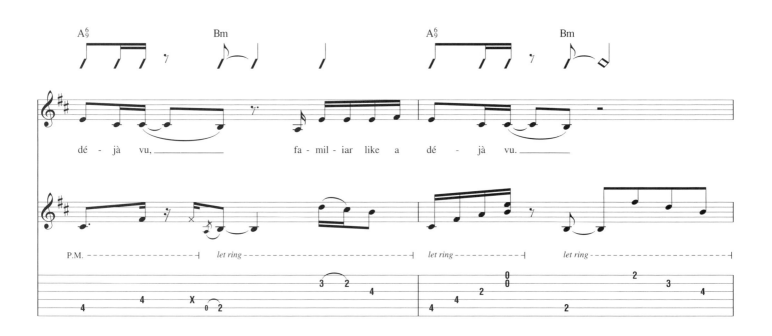

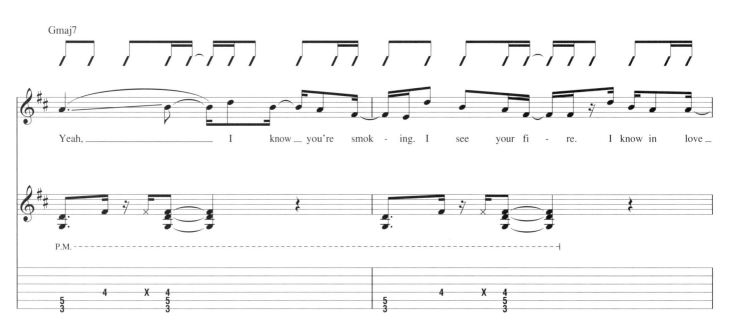

you've been giv-ing it up. ___ So do I qual-i-fy? Qual-i-fy. Qual-i-fy.

Chorus

Qual-i-fy. Qual-i-fy. I ___ wan-na be the one who will help you move on ___ from Mis-ter

Lone-li-ness liv-ing in the kitch-en of your home. I'm hop-ing you can feel me. I'm hop-ing that I don't run out of

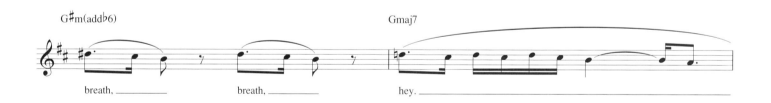

breath, ___ breath, ___ hey.

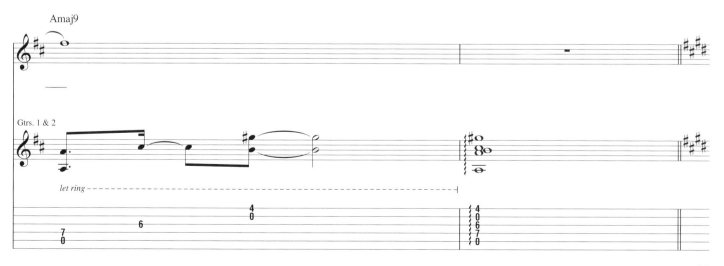

Interlude

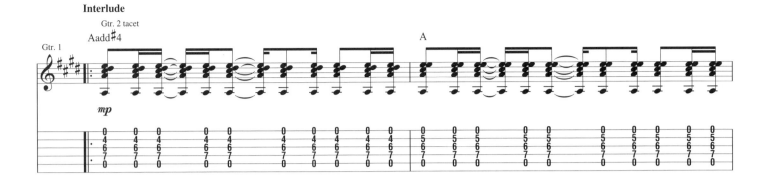

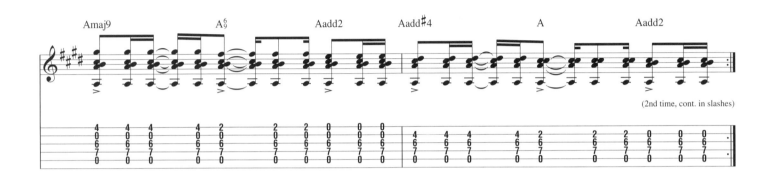

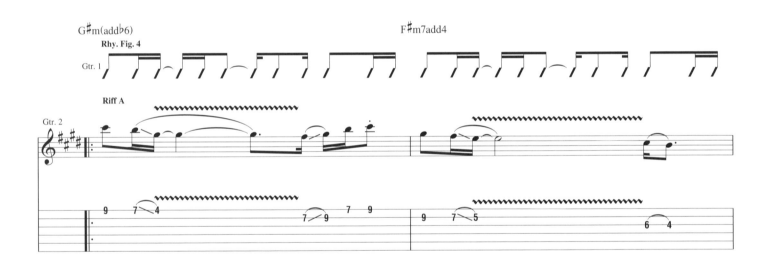

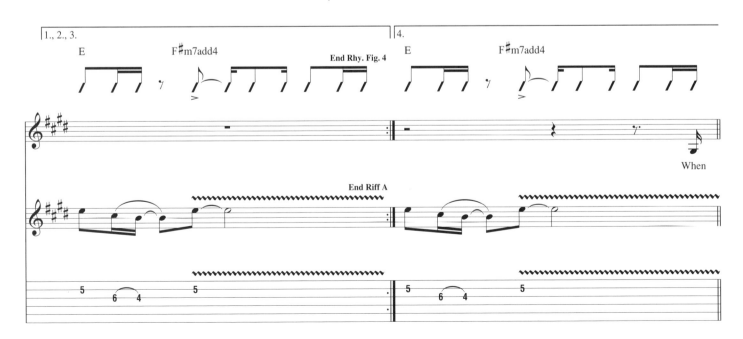

Outro

Gtr. 1: w/ Rhy. Fig. 4 (2 times)
Gtr. 2: w/ Riff A (2 times)

our two hands _ are linked to - geth - er with an am - per - sand, it's my _ kind of

di - a - gram. _ When our _ sore _ eyes _ are lined up

side by _ side, _ well, I'm a hap - py man. _ Yes, I'm a

Gtr. 1: w/ Rhy. Fig. 4 (last meas.)   Gtr. 1: w/ Rhy. Fig. 4

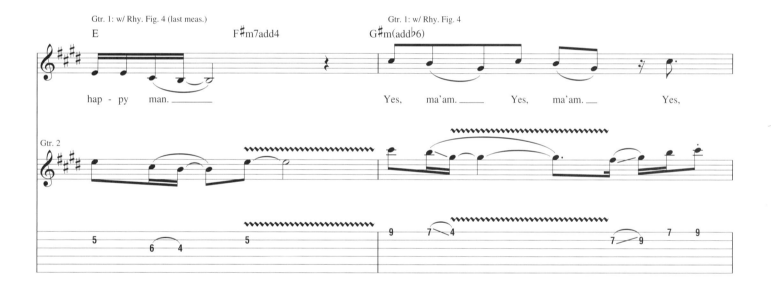

hap - py man. _ Yes, ma'am. _ Yes, ma'am. _ Yes,

Gtr. 2

ma'am. _ I am think - ing a - bout _ you. _

IN YOUR HANDS

Words and Music by
Jason Mraz

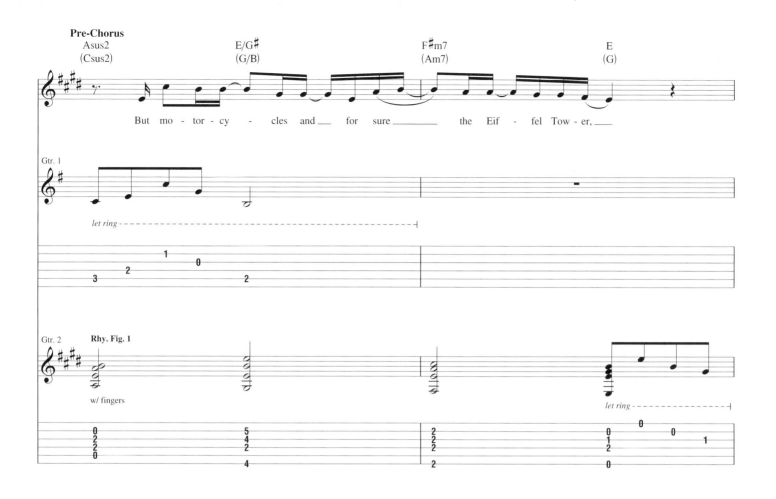

But mo - tor - cy - cles and __ for sure __ the Eif - fel Tow - er, __

Gtr. 1

let ring -

Gtr. 2 **Rhy. Fig. 1**

w/ fingers

let ring - - - - - - - - - - - - - -

they were made __ for two. __ A dou - ble bed __ has nev - er

let ring - - - - - - - - - - - - - - - - -

let ring - w/ thumb

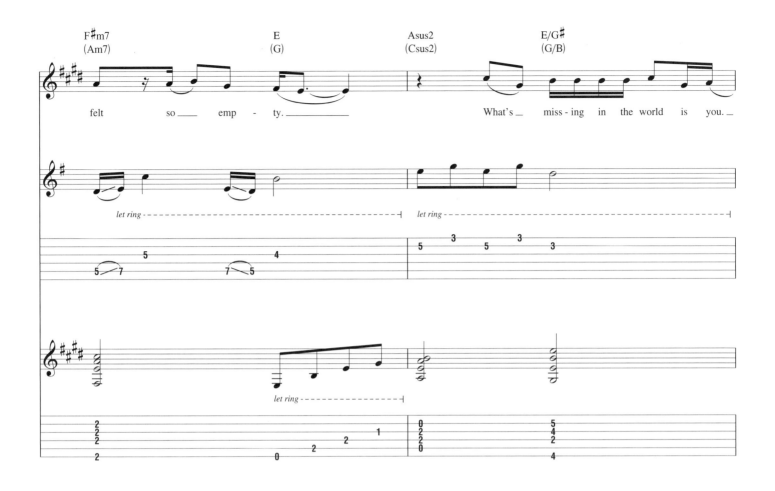

felt so ___ emp-ty. ___ What's ___ miss-ing in the world is you. ___

So I'll leave it in your ___ hands ___

End Rhy. Fig. 1

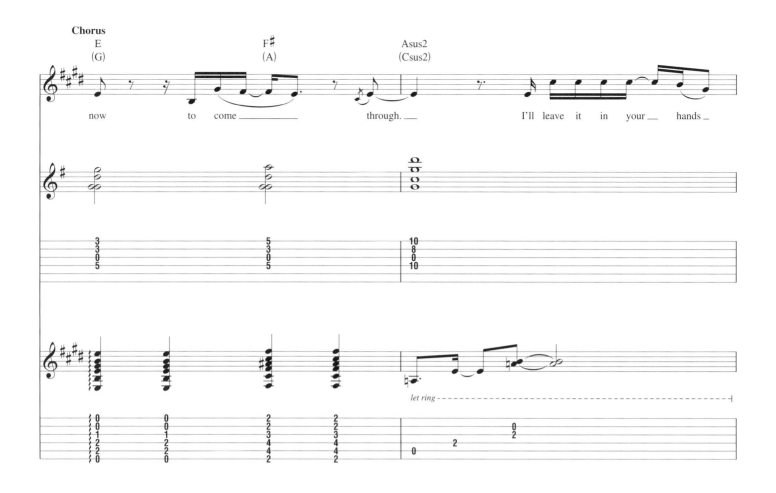

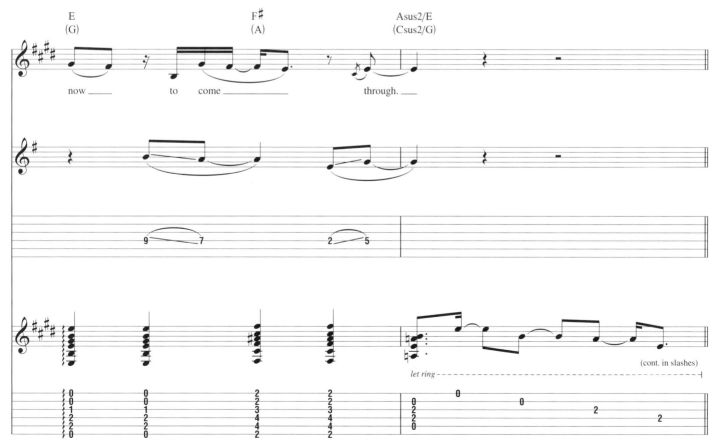

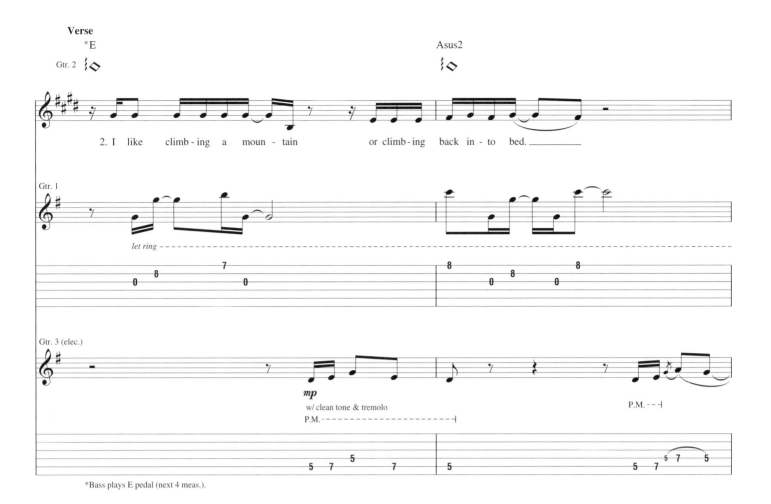

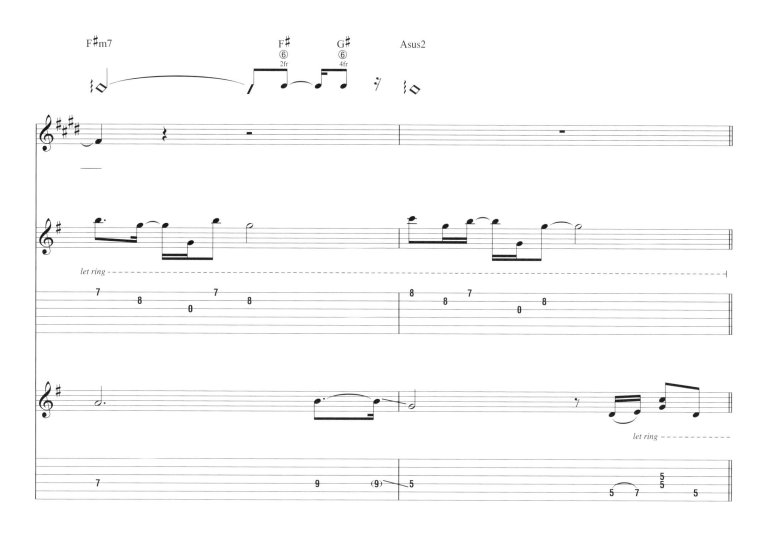

Pre-Chorus

Gtr. 2: w/ Rhy. Fig. 1

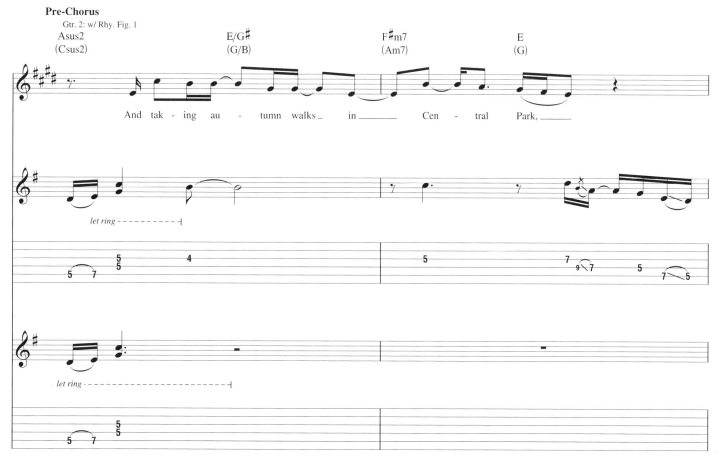

And tak - ing au - tumn walks _ in _____ Cen - tral Park, _____

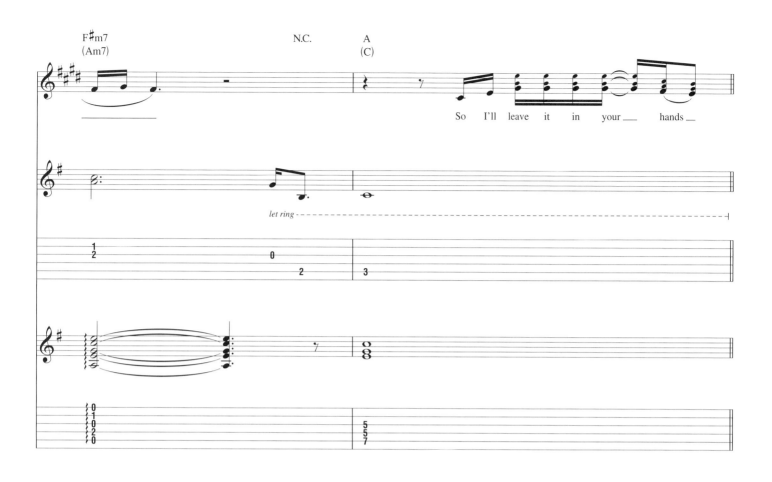

So I'll leave it in your ___ hands ___

let ring -

% Chorus

now   to come _____ through. ___   I'll leave it in your ___ hands ___

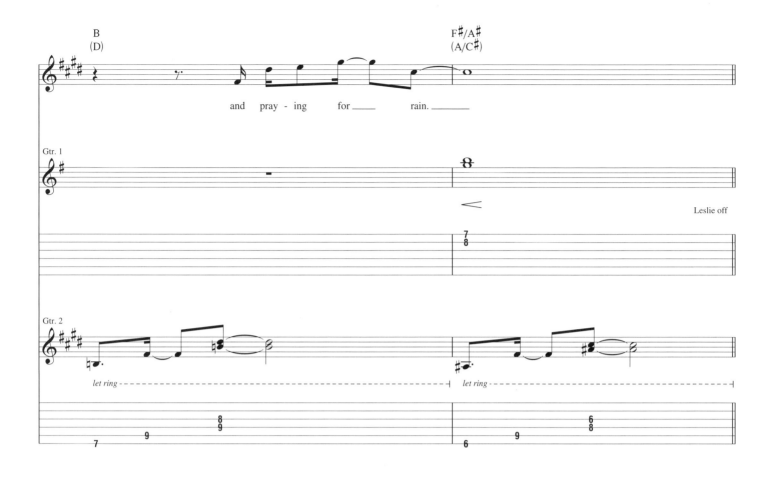

and pray - ing for ___ rain. ___

Gtr. 1

Leslie off

Gtr. 2

let ring

let ring

Pre-Chorus

Asus2   E/G#   F#m7   E   Asus2   E/G#
(Csus2) (G/B)   (Am7)   (G) (Csus2) (G/B)

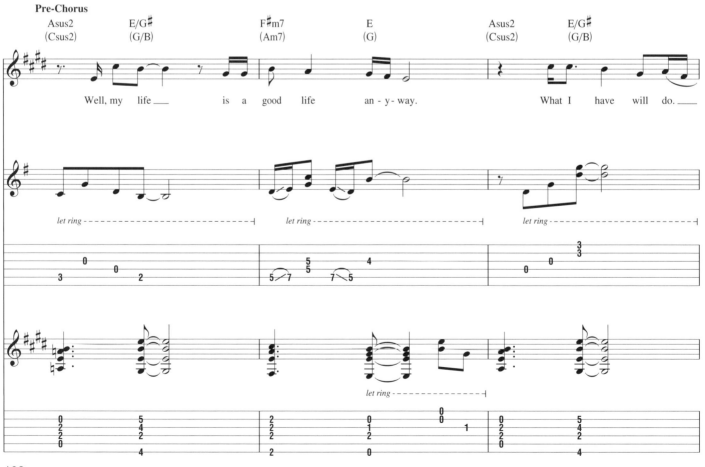

Well, my life ___ is a good life an-y-way. What I have will do. ___

let ring

let ring

let ring

let ring

So I'll leave it in your ___ hands ___

Coda

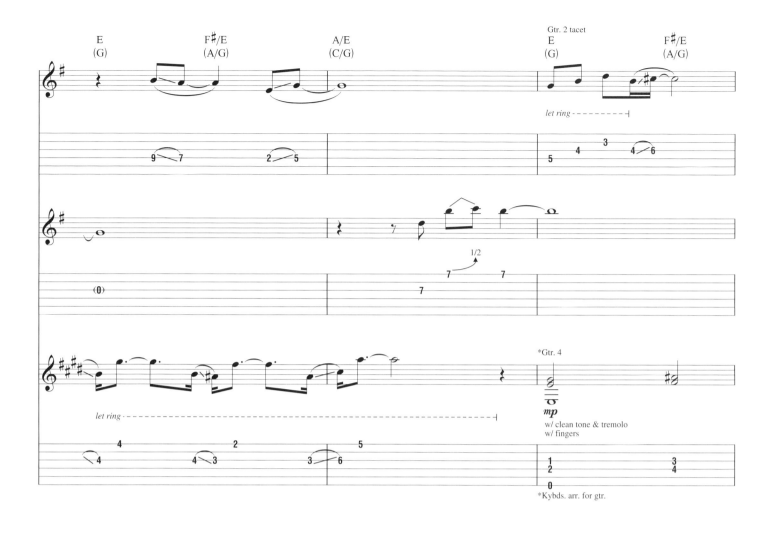

105

BE HONEST

Words and Music by
Jason Mraz and Michael Natter

Drop D tuning:
(low to high) D-A-D-G-B-E

Intro
Moderately ♩ = 112

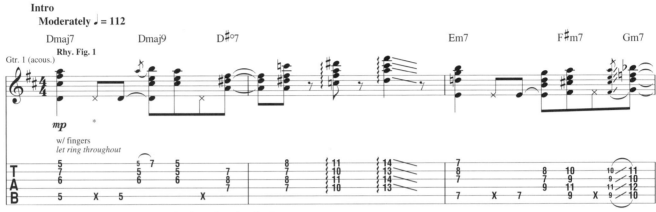

*X indicates to lightly hit string w/ R.H. (throughout).

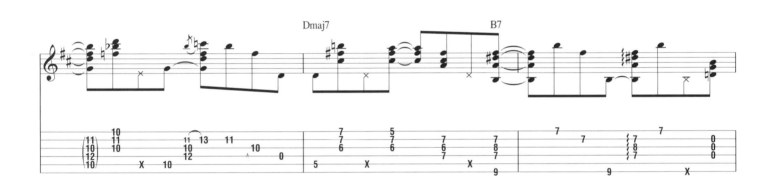

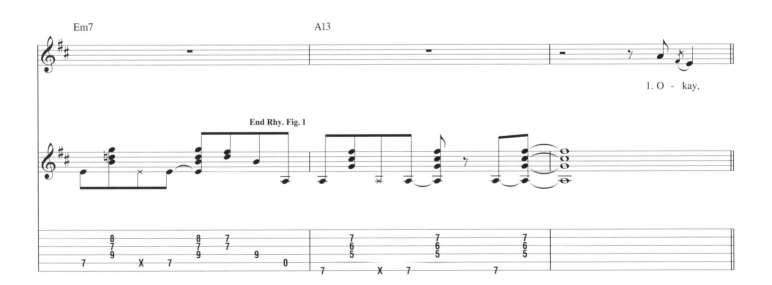

1. O - kay,

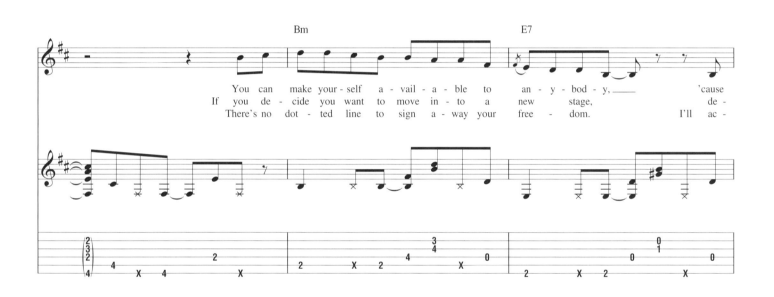

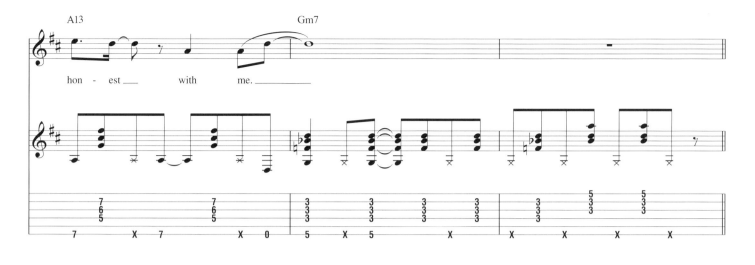

Bridge

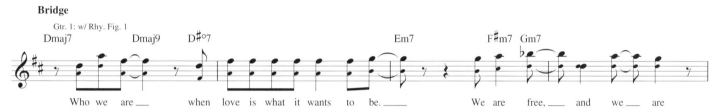

Interlude

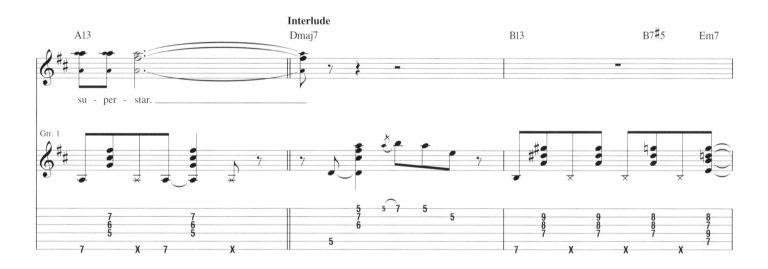

D.S. al Coda

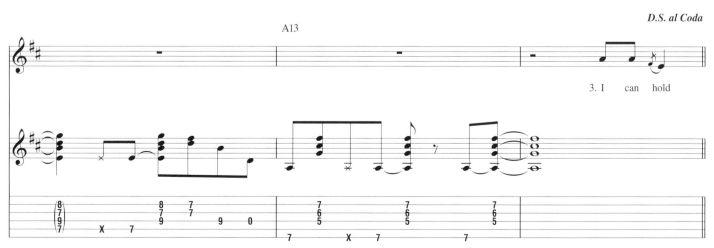

Coda

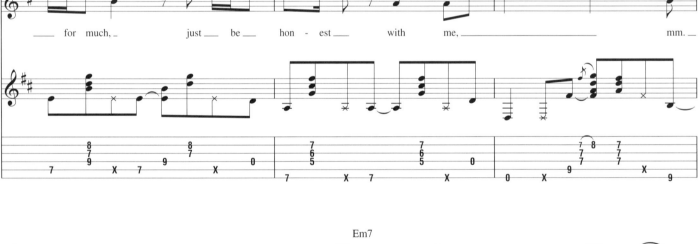

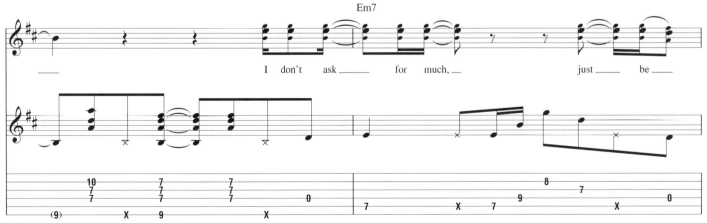

THE WORLD AS I SEE IT

Words and Music by
Jason Mraz and Rick Nowels

see it is a re- mark - a- ble place. __ Ev- 'ry man __

makes a dif- f'rence and ev- 'ry moth- er's child __ is a saint. __ From a bird's __

__ eye __ view __ I can see we are spi - ral- ing __ down in grav- i- ty.

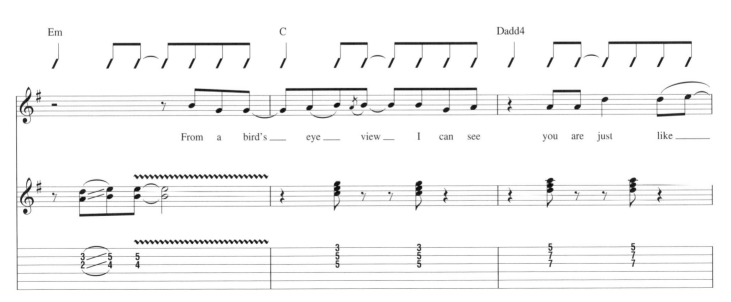

From a bird's __ eye __ view __ I can see you are just like __

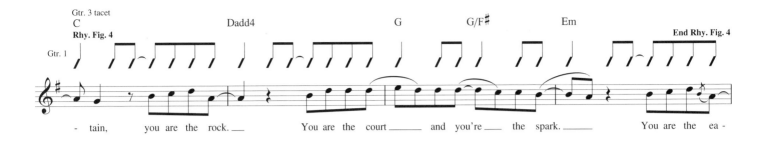

Gtr. 3 tacet

C   Dadd4   G   G/F#   Em

Rhy. Fig. 4   End Rhy. Fig. 4

Gtr. 1

-tain,   you are the rock. ___   You are the court ___ and you're ___ the spark. ___   You are the ea-

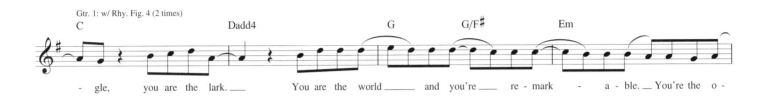

Gtr. 1: w/ Rhy. Fig. 4 (2 times)

C   Dadd4   G   G/F#   Em

-gle,   you are the lark. ___   You are the world ___ and you're ___ re- mark - a - ble. ___ You're the o-

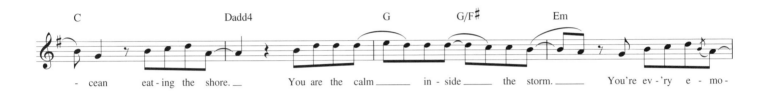

C   Dadd4   G   G/F#   Em

-cean   eat- ing the shore. ___   You are the calm ___ in - side ___ the storm. ___   You're ev -'ry e - mo-

C   Dadd4   Em7

Gtr. 1

-tion   you can en - dure. ___   You are the world ___ and the world is ___ yours. ___   It's not ___ hard ___

Chorus

Gtr. 1: w/ Rhy. Fig. 2 (2 times)
Gtr. 2: w/ Riff A (2 times)
Gtr. 3: w/ Riff C (2 times)

Am   G

___ for me to love you,   hard ___ for me to love you.   No, ___ it's not a dif- fi - cult thing. ___

Am

No,   it's   not... ___
___   It's   not   hard ___ for me to love you,   hard ___ for me to love you

Gtr. 3: w/ Riff B (3 times)

G   Am

un - con - di - tion - al - ly.   No,   it's   not ___ hard ___ for me to love ___ you.
    It's   not ___ hard ___ for me to love you,   hard ___

I'M COMING OVER

Words and Music by
Jason Mraz and Mike Daly

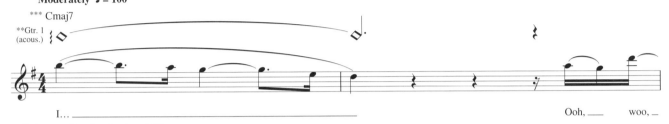

*Drop D tuning, down 2 1/2 steps, capo II:
(low to high) A-E-A-D-F♯-B

Intro
Moderately ♩ = 100

*** Cmaj7

**Gtr. 1
(acous.)

I...   Ooh, __ woo, __

*Equivalent to Drop D tuning, down 1 1/2 steps, no capo.
**Two gtrs. arr. for one
***See top of page for chord diagrams pertaining to rhythm slashes.

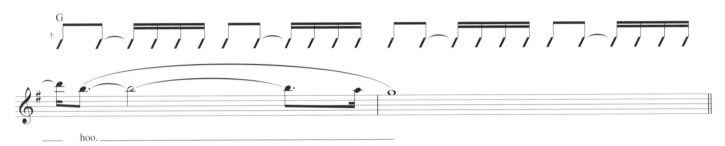

G

__ hoo. _____

†For chords in rhythm slashes, play only bottom note of chord on beats 1 and 3 (till end).

Verse

Dm6   C

Rhy. Fig. 1

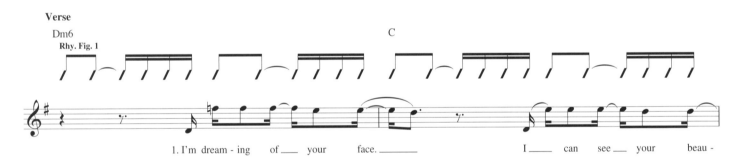

1. I'm dream-ing of __ your face. _____ I can see __ your beau-

G   End Rhy. Fig. 1

-ty through ten and a half __ thou-sand yes-ter-days. __

Gtr. 1: w/ Rhy. Fig. 1

Dm6   C

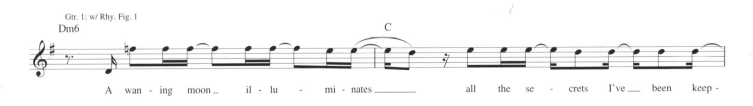

A wan-ing moon __ il-lu-mi-nates _____ all the se-crets I've been keep-

-ing   and   cast - ing off ___ of   my   bal - co - ny. ___   Oh, ___

Pre-Chorus

I,   I,   I,   I, ___   I, ___

I   hope ___ you   no - tice ___

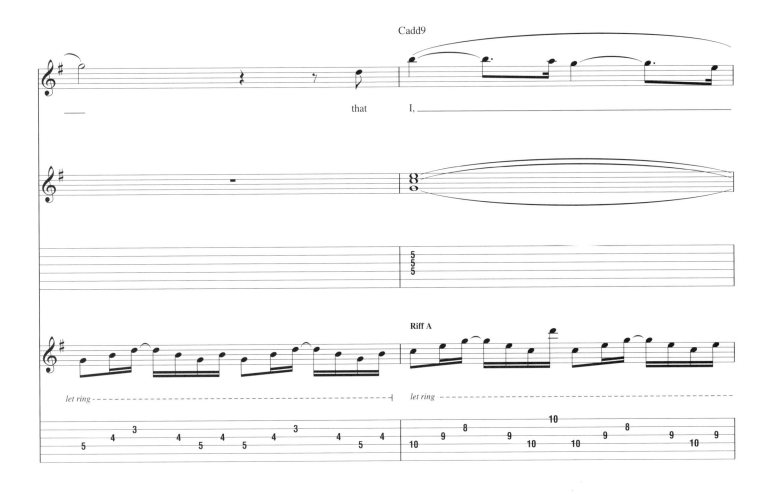

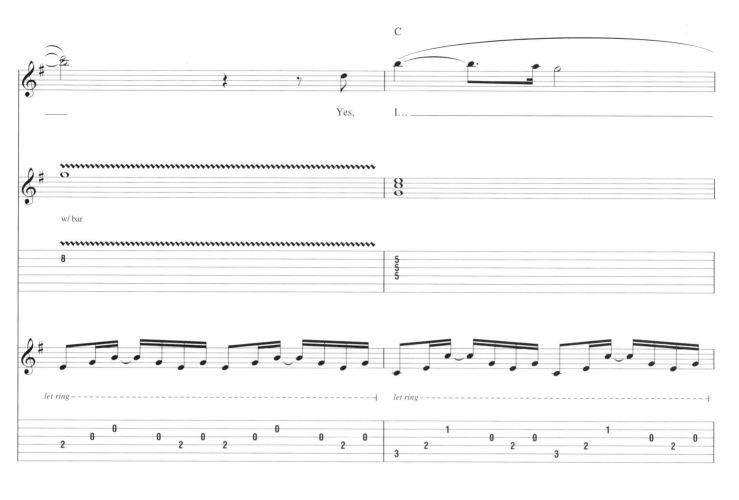

Yes, I...

w/ bar

let ring

Chorus
Gtr. 2 tacet
G
Rhy. Fig. 2
Gtr. 1

Dadd4

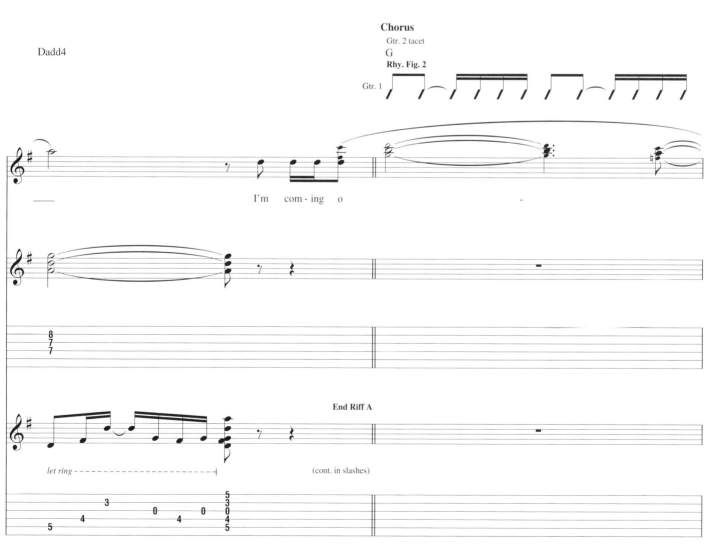

I'm com-ing o

End Riff A

let ring

(cont. in slashes)

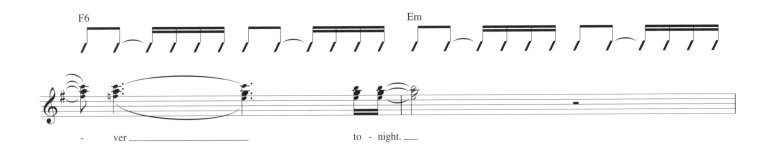

-ver _____ to - night. ___

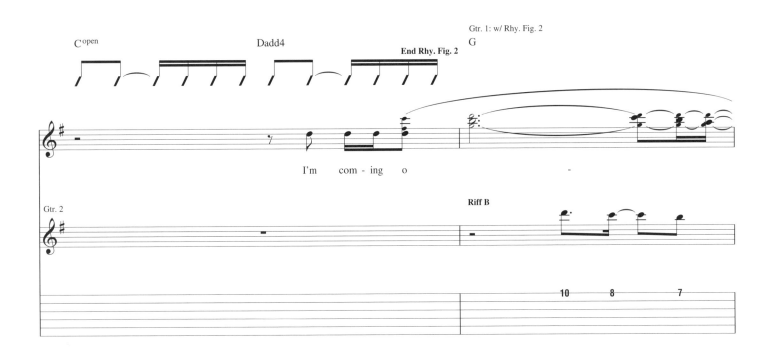

I'm com - ing o ___

-ver _____ to - night. ___ I hope you

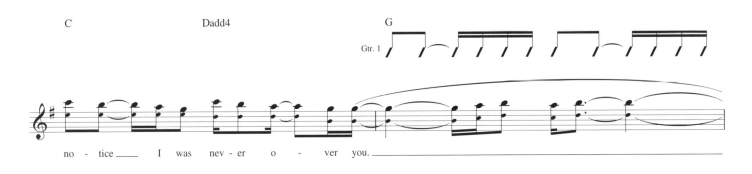

no - tice ___ I was nev - er o - ver you. ___

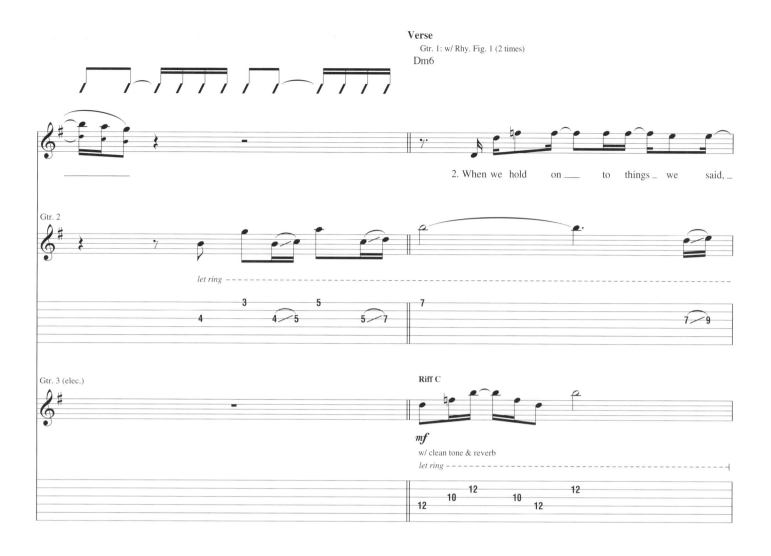

2. When we hold on — to things — we said, —

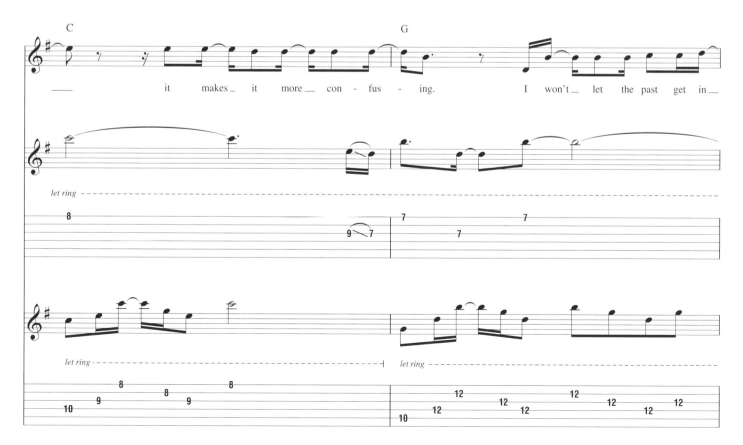

— it makes — it more — con - fus - ing.   I won't — let the past get in —

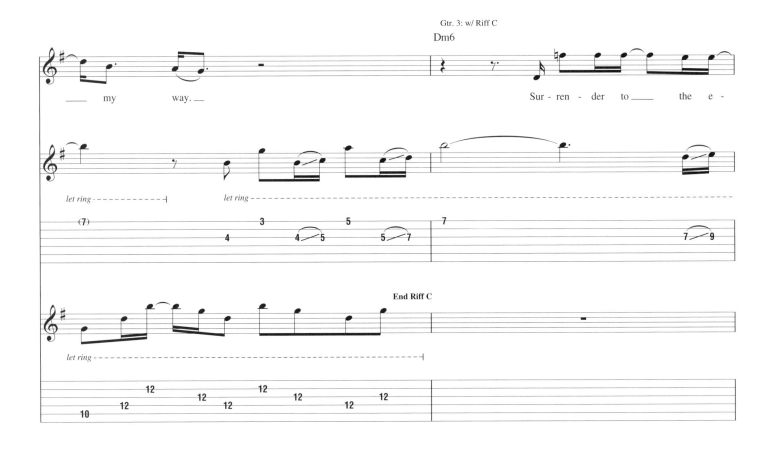

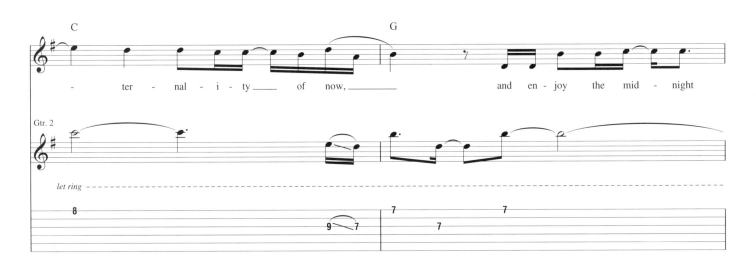

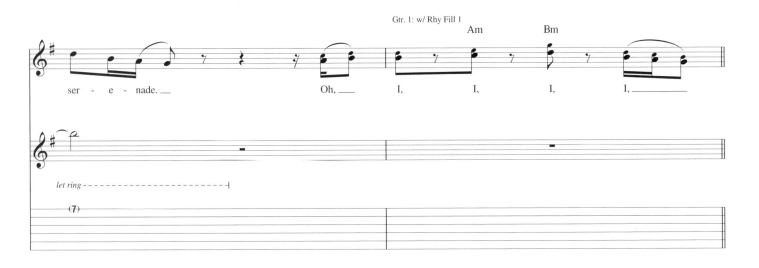

Pre-Chorus

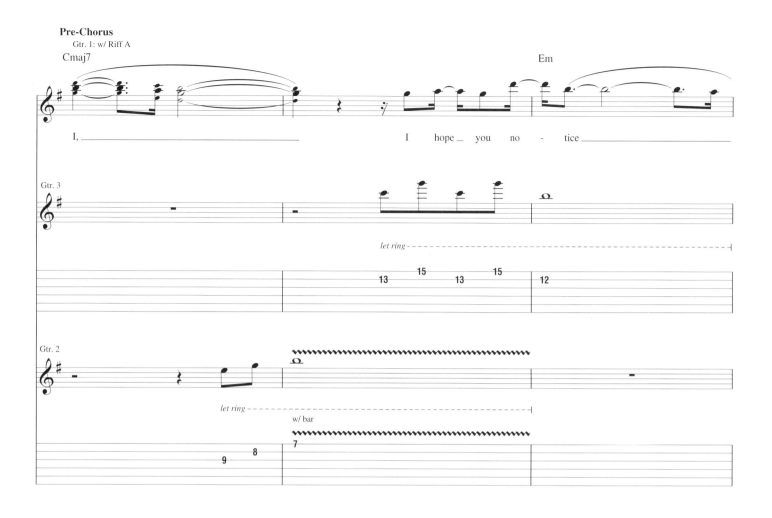

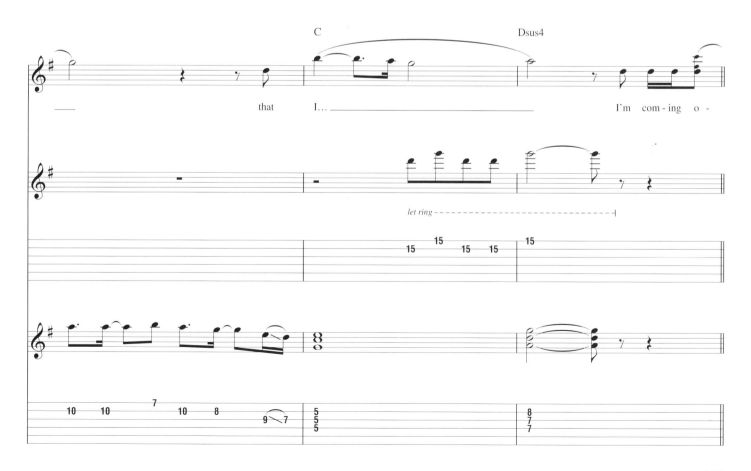

God, I love this. If ev-er there was a place that I could stay,

I found it. I, I, I, I,

Pre-Chorus

I, I hope you no-tice

let ring

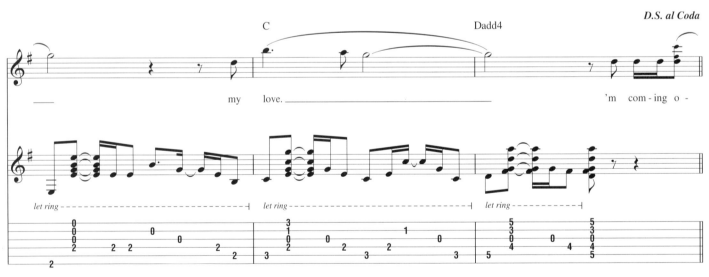

my love. 'm com-ing o-

let ring

D.S. al Coda

✛ **Coda**

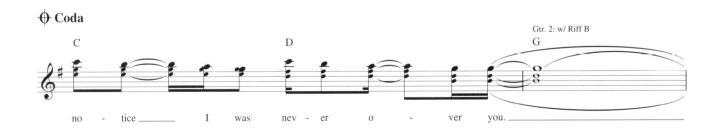

no-tice I was nev-er o-ver you.

Outro

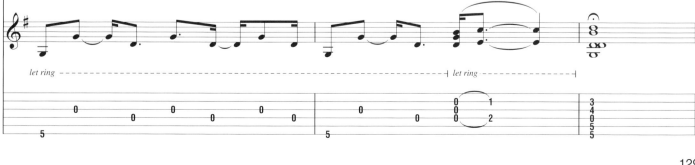

GUITAR NOTATION LEGEND

Guitar music can be notated three different ways: on a *musical staff*, in *tablature*, and in *rhythm slashes*.

RHYTHM SLASHES are written above the staff. Strum chords in the rhythm indicated. Use the chord diagrams found at the top of the first page of the transcription for the appropriate chord voicings. Round noteheads indicate single notes.

THE MUSICAL STAFF shows pitches and rhythms and is divided by bar lines into measures. Pitches are named after the first seven letters of the alphabet.

TABLATURE graphically represents the guitar fingerboard. Each horizontal line represents a string, and each number represents a fret.

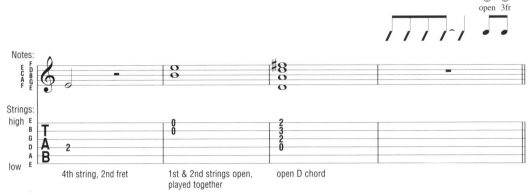

4th string, 2nd fret   1st & 2nd strings open, played together   open D chord

HALF-STEP BEND: Strike the note and bend up 1/2 step.

BEND AND RELEASE: Strike the note and bend up as indicated, then release back to the original note. Only the first note is struck.

HAMMER-ON: Strike the first (lower) note with one finger, then sound the higher note (on the same string) with another finger by fretting it without picking.

TRILL: Very rapidly alternate between the notes indicated by continuously hammering on and pulling off.

PICK SCRAPE: The edge of the pick is rubbed down (or up) the string, producing a scratchy sound.

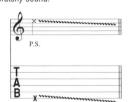

TREMOLO PICKING: The note is picked as rapidly and continuously as possible.

WHOLE-STEP BEND: Strike the note and bend up one step.

PRE-BEND: Bend the note as indicated, then strike it.

PULL-OFF: Place both fingers on the notes to be sounded. Strike the first note and without picking, pull the finger off to sound the second (lower) note.

TAPPING: Hammer ("tap") the fret indicated with the pick-hand index or middle finger and pull off to the note fretted by the fret hand.

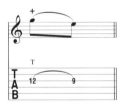

MUFFLED STRINGS: A percussive sound is produced by laying the fret hand across the string(s) without depressing, and striking them with the pick hand.

VIBRATO BAR DIVE AND RETURN: The pitch of the note or chord is dropped a specified number of steps (in rhythm), then returned to the original pitch.

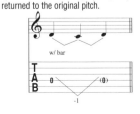

GRACE NOTE BEND: Strike the note and immediately bend up as indicated.

VIBRATO: The string is vibrated by rapidly bending and releasing the note with the fretting hand.

LEGATO SLIDE: Strike the first note and then slide the same fret-hand finger up or down to the second note. The second note is not struck.

NATURAL HARMONIC: Strike the note while the fret-hand lightly touches the string directly over the fret indicated.

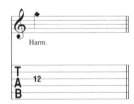

PALM MUTING: The note is partially muted by the pick hand lightly touching the string(s) just before the bridge.

VIBRATO BAR SCOOP: Depress the bar just before striking the note, then quickly release the bar.

SLIGHT (MICROTONE) BEND: Strike the note and bend up 1/4 step.

WIDE VIBRATO: The pitch is varied to a greater degree by vibrating with the fretting hand.

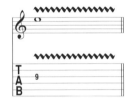

SHIFT SLIDE: Same as legato slide, except the second note is struck.

PINCH HARMONIC: The note is fretted normally and a harmonic is produced by adding the edge of the thumb or the tip of the index finger of the pick hand to the normal pick attack.

RAKE: Drag the pick across the strings indicated with a single motion.

VIBRATO BAR DIP: Strike the note and then immediately drop a specified number of steps, then release back to the original pitch.

STRUM & SING WITH

cherry lane
music company

GUITAR

SARA BAREILLES
00102354..$12.99

ZAC BROWN BAND
02501620..$12.99

COLBIE CAILLAT
02501725..$14.99

CAMPFIRE FOLK SONGS
02500686..$10.99

CHRISTMAS CAROLS
02500631..$6.95

COUNTRY
02500755..$9.95

JOHN DENVER COLLECTION
02500632..$9.95

50 CHILDREN'S SONGS
02500825..$7.95

THE 5 CHORD SONGBOOK
02501718..$9.99

FOLK SONGS
02501482..$9.99

FOLK/ROCK FAVORITES
02501669..$9.99

40 POP/ROCK HITS
02500633..$9.95

THE 4 CHORD SONGBOOK
02501533..$10.99

HITS OF THE '60S
02501138..$10.95

HITS OF THE '70S
02500871..$9.99

HYMNS
02501125..$8.99

JACK JOHNSON
02500858..$14.99

DAVE MATTHEWS BAND
02501078..$10.95

JOHN MAYER
02501636..$10.99

INGRID MICHAELSON
02501634..$10.99

THE MOST REQUESTED SONGS
02501748..$10.99

JASON MRAZ
02501452..$14.99

ROCK BALLADS
02500872..$9.95

THE 6 CHORD SONGBOOK
02502277..$10.99

UKULELE

COLBIE CAILLAT
02501731..$10.99

JOHN DENVER
02501694..$10.99

JACK JOHNSON
02501752..$10.99

JOHN MAYER
02501706..$10.99

INGRID MICHAELSON
02501741..$10.99

THE MOST REQUESTED SONGS
02501453..$10.99

JASON MRAZ
02501753..$14.99

SING-ALONG SONGS
02501710..$10.99

See your local music dealer or contact:

cherry lane
music company

EXCLUSIVELY DISTRIBUTED BY
HAL•LEONARD®
CORPORATION

7777 W. BLUEMOUND RD. P.O. BOX 13819 MILWAUKEE, WI 53213

Prices, content, and availability subject to change
without notice.

0512

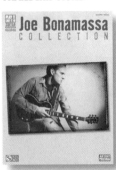
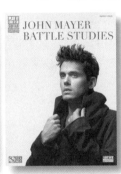